IRREFUTABLE PROOF THAT JESUS IS THE MESSIAH

Dr. Charles A. Crane

2020

Irrefutable Proof that Jesus Is the Messiah
is available at special quantity discounts for bulk purchase for sales promotions, premiums, fund-raising, and educational needs.

For details write:
Endurance Press, 577 N Cardigan Ave, Star ID 83669.
Visit Endurance Press' website at *www.endurancepress.com*

Irrefutable Proof that Jesus Is the Messiah

PUBLISHED BY ENDURANCE PRESS
577 N Cardigan Ave
Star, ID 83669 U.S.A.

All views expressed within are the view of the author and do not necessarily reflect the views of the publisher.

© Dr. Charles A. Crane 2020
All rights reserved. Except for brief excerpts for review purposes,
no part of this book may be
reproduced or used in any form without
prior written permission from the publisher.
ISBN 9781733550352

"Scripture quotations are from the ESV® Bible (The Holy Bible, English Standard Version®), copyright © 2001 by Crossway, a publishing ministry of Good News Publishers. Used by permission. All rights reserved."

L.C.
Printed in the U.S.A.

TABLE OF CONTENTS

Introduction 7
    The Bible: A Book about Jesus 9
    My Bible 11

Chapter One—Manuscript Evidence for the Bible, John 10:35
    The Great Synagogue 13
    The Bible. 14
    Moses and Seventy Leaders 15
    The Septuagint 15
    The Sanhedrin. 16
    The Dead Sea Scrolls and the Old Testament 16
    The Olivet Discourse. 18
    Metropolitan Samuel 19
    How Firm a Foundation. 21
    The Perfect Church 22
    John the Baptist 23
    Summary. 23

Chapter Two—Prophecy as Proof that Jesus Is the Messiah, Luke 24:44
    353 Prophecies about Jesus Are Quoted in the
        Old Testament, the List 25
    353 Prophecies Fulfilled in Jesus Christ, the List of Where
        These Are Quoted in the New Testament 26
    Jesus As the "I Am" 37
    Concerning Himself. 39
    Prophetic Predictions. 41
    Consider Some of These Actual Prophecies. 43

Genesis... 43
- The tree in prophecy ... 43
- Aaron's rod that budded... 44
- The Branch prophecies... 44

Psalms 22 and 88... 48
- Psalm 22... 48
- Psalm 88... 50

Speaking to and hearing God... 52
- Isaiah 7:14; 9:6-7; 52—53 ... 52
- Isaiah 7:14... 52
- Isaiah 9:6—7... 53
- Isaiah 52 and 53... 54

Eternal God Whose Power upholds ... 58
- Daniel 9... 59

The Book of Books... 62
- Micah 5:2-3... 63
- Zechariah 12—14 ... 63

Chapter Three—The Resurrection As Proof that Jesus Is the Messiah, 0I Corinthians 15:1-8

The Witnesses to the Resurrection Listed in I Corinthians 15... 67

A List of Additional Resurrection Appearances ... 69

Pentecost ... 70

The First Few Weeks in Jerusalem ... 72

Samaria and Beyond... 73

Conversion of Saul and the Beginning of World Missions ... 73

The Gentiles are Being Evangelized Now ... 73

The End of the First Century... 75

The First to Fourth Centuries 76

Conclusion—What Do We Know for Sure? Three Truths:

Truth One—The Bible Is Accurate 79

The Anvil of God's Word 79

Truth Two—Prophecy Proves Who Jesus Was and Is 80

Truth Three—The Resurrection Gives Irrefutable Proof
that Jesus Is the Promised Messiah 81

The Cross Was His Own 81

A Call to Faith 83

Jerry McCauley 86

Marcia 86

Mike 87

What a Friend We Have in Jesus 89

The Deadline 91

Appendix 95

Dr. Charles A. Crane

Charles A. Crane was raised on a cattle ranch in the foothills of the Cascade Mountains of Oregon. He was five days old his first day in church and has been there ever since. He has been heavily involved in the work of the church all of his life. He began preaching weekly at age nineteen and was ordained following graduation from college in 1962. For twenty-eight years he served as a preaching minister until he became President of Boise Bible College in 1990.

His education includes the Bachelor of Sacred Literature degree from Northwest College of the Bible, Portland, Oregon; the M.A. and M.Div. degrees from Lincoln Christian Seminary, Lincoln, Illinois; the Doctor of Ministry degree from Luther-Rice Seminary of Jacksonville, Florida, and Atlanta, Georgia; and CPEC from St. Luke's Hospital, Boise, Idaho.

He has taught college and seminary in the areas of Theology, Church Administration, Psychology, Textual Criticism and Practical Ministries.

He has worked in church planting and world missions and been a guest lecturer to missionaries in Germany, France, India, and Zimbabwe, Africa. He has led three leadership training clinics for indigenous church leaders in Zimbabwe. He was the keynote speaker for a conference of missionaries from five African nations in Harare, Africa.

He is the author of many books, including *Christianity and Mormonism: From Bondage to Freedom*, *The Bible and Mormon Scriptures Compared* (a best seller), *A Practical Guide to Soul Winning* (a college text book), *Do You Know What the Mormon Church Teaches?*, *Mormon Missionaries in Flight*, *Ashamed of Joseph—Mormon Foundations Crumble*, *Christian Money Management*, *The Bible: The True and Reliable Word of God*, *The Families of Man, Biblically and Archaeologically Traced from Noah Until Today*, *Adventures of a Young Preacher*, as well as numerous articles for magazines, and many scholarly papers for publication on a variety of subjects.

He is in the film The God Makers, a documentary on Mormonism, as well as many educational videos on the cults, personal finance, and church administration, which are used for adult education. He participated in a weekly nationwide television program entitled Which Way America for two years.

Dr. Crane retired as president of Boise Bible College in 2007, and is currently serving as Chancellor. He is also on the staff of Eagle Christian Church, Eagle, Idaho. He has served three terms on the Board of Directors of the North American Christian Convention, and served on two different college boards for a total of twelve years, was a trustee six years as well as chairman of the Navajo Christian Churches Mission Board one year. He served six years as a director of the Intermountain Christian Convention and as president one year.

He has traveled extensively in Africa, Europe, Asia Minor, and the Middle East, as well as in India, Canada, Mexico, the Caribbean and South America. For fifty years he has led educational tours of Israel and throughout the Middle East, Europe, and Africa.

He has a variety of interests including ancient biblical manuscripts, equipping church members to use their God-given talents, writing, reading, fountain pen collecting and restoration, piloting a private airplane, and travel. But the focus of his life has always been the church of Christ.

Introduction

Is there irrefutable proof that Jesus is who He claimed to be—the Messiah and the Savior of humanity? The answer to this question is a definite yes. Two thousand years ago, a young teacher, named Jesus, made some very bold and even audacious claims about who He was and how we should live our lives. He announced Himself to be the Messiah, the fulfillment of all of the prophecies of the Old Testament scriptures, and even the Savior of all humanity.

While others have made, and some still do, make similar claims, His were unique in that they were demonstrated to be true by a huge number of deeds, evidence, and miraculous acts. So convincing were these proofs that His followers devoted their lives to proclaiming these facts, and unhesitatingly submitted to death for doing so. Hundreds and thousands of others were witnesses to this evidence as well, and their lives were changed accordingly. This is still happening today.

But can this evidences still be convincing, in this time so far removed from that day, and with our advanced education, and culture? The answer is a resounding "yes," and the purpose of this book is to present the evidence that you may believe as well. Here are a few modern examples of how convincing the evidence is. This information is extensive but is limited to key facts so as to be easily read and understood.

Josh McDowell was a young agnostic headed for law school. He had grown weary of debating about the accuracy of the claims of Christianity. When challenged to intellectually examine these claims, he bent himself to the task of forming a rigorous disproof of what he saw as the falsehood of

Christianity. But, the result of his research was that he ended up proving that the claims of Christ were true.

To his credit, he was honest with himself, bowed his knee, and submitted to Jesus as his Lord. His initial work was in a book of lecture notes used in his class entitled Christianity: Hoax or History?, and the book he later wrote from these sources is entitled, Evidence that Demands a Verdict. This work is still being widely read and updated, remaining a staple of Christian reading today. Instead of being a lawyer he has devoted himself to a ministry of spreading this gospel truth and his life has borne lots of fruit for good.

Another example is Lee Strobel who was a seasoned journalist and legal affairs editor for the Chicago Tribune. He was well trained at Yale, and he was a committed atheist. He became alarmed and concerned by his wife's new found Christian belief. Like McDowell, he devoted himself to convincing her of the falsehood of Jesus' claims, but his diligent work instead ended up convincing him of their truth and he is today an effective Christian evangelist. His first book, The Case for Christ, is an account of his journey to Christian faith.

Many other modern examples could be given since these experiences are not rare. They are examples of current day intelligent, clear-thinking, and intellectually honest people, who see that the facts support—even demand—a conclusion: Christianity is unique in that it does not require us to "leave our brains at the door," but rather stands up to the highest levels of investigation. Towering intellectuals such as C. S. Lewis and multitudes of others are proof of this. Christianity is a faith founded on facts.

Unfortunately, many have never had access to this information. Some who know the truth of the matter still reject Christ for other reasons. The purpose of this book is to provide information that is positive and irrefutable proof that Jesus is the Christ and the Savior of all who will accept Him.

So this leaves us with primarily two reasons that people still reject Jesus as the Christ: either they have never been presented with the facts, and had an opportunity to examine them, or if they have they have hardened their hearts against these truths, not wanting them in their lives with the consequences that they would bring. This is the difference between being unable to believe and being unwilling to believe[1] (John 3:19-20).[2]

The purpose for this book is to give the irrefutable proof that Jesus is the Messiah. This information today has been fully proven. If you struggle with believing, carefully consider what the Creator of humanity, Jesus Himself, says that it is because "their works are evil" (John 3:19).

Sixty years in ministry has confirmed this diagnosis over and over again. There is a part of our lives that we do not want to submit to the lordship of Christ, therefore, people reject Him. If you still have trouble believing in Christ, please examine your heart and be honest with yourself—is Jesus unbelievable, or is it that you are unwilling to let Him direct your life?

We will begin with the Bible and examine its history and teachings. We will examine ancient Biblical manuscript evidence, and the history of the Bible's writing. And next we will look at its prophecies about Jesus, and finally look at the proof that we as humans are eternal and all of us will live forever.

First, it is helpful to understand that Jesus is the theme of the entire Bible:

THE BIBLE IS A BOOK ABOUT JESUS

Genesis—He is the Promised Seed
Exodus—He is the Passover Lamb
Leviticus—He is the Scapegoat
Numbers—He is the Brazen Serpent
Deuteronomy—He is the giver of the Law
Joshua—He is the Savior of his people
Judges—He is the Great Judge
Ruth—He is the Kinsman and Redeemer

---

1   Scripture quotations will be given from The English Standard Version unless otherwise noted.

2   The English Standard Version does not capitalize the personal pronouns referring to Jesus Christ, but I do, you may note this difference. Some other translations do capitalize them when referring to Jesus.

I–II Samuel—He is the Prophet, Priest and King

I–II Kings—He is King of Kings and Lord of Lords

I–II Chronicles—He is the Great Historian, keeping a record of His people

Ezra—He is the Builder of the Temple

Nehemiah—He is the Builder of the walls, protector of His people

Esther—He is the Savior of the Jewish Nation

Job—He is the Friend that sticks closer than a brother

Psalms—He is the Song of the Ages

Proverbs—He is the Truth

Ecclesiastes—He is the Great Preacher

Song of Solomon—He is the Great Lover of his bride, Israel and the Church

Isaiah—He is the Suffering servant saving His people

Jeremiah—He is standing at the gate of the city saying, "Is it nothing to you who pass by?"

Ezekiel—He is the Nation's restorer to Israel

Daniel—He is the Stone cut out of the mountains, without hands, that fills the whole earth

Hosea—He is the spurned Lover

Minor Prophets—Promised Messiah coming to Bethlehem of Judea

Matthew—He is King of Kings and Lord of Lords, fulfilling every Old Testament prophecy of Him.

Mark—He is the Suffering Servant

Luke—He is the Son of Man, Savior

John—He is the Son of God, Savior

Acts—He is the Power of the Church and Gospel

Romans—He is the Gospel of Salvation

I–II Corinthians—He is the Restorer of the fallen nature

Galatians—He is the one who rends the Temple Veil ending the Old Covenant

Ephesians—He is the Lord of the Church

Philippians—He is our all Sufficiency
Colossians—He is the Shadow that now has come bodily
I-II Thessalonians—He is our soon coming King
I-II Timothy—He is the Overseer of the Church
Titus—He is the Savior uplifting humanity
Philemon—He is the Redeemer of rebellious slaves
Hebrews—He is the New Covenant, Prophet, Priest and King
James—He is the power of the Gospel for good works
I-II Peter—His suffering is our example of how to live with our own suffering
I-II-III John—He is the source of abiding Love
Revelation—He is coming again

Although you might assign a somewhat different theme to some of the 66 Bible books than given here, yet the point is clear that the Bible is full of Jesus. The Old Testament has about 500 prophecies about Jesus and His life. The New Testament quotes at least 353 of these Old Testament prophecies about Jesus. We will show that in total there are about 7,000 references to Jesus in our 39 Old Testament books.

MY BIBLE

And should my soul be torn with grief
    Upon my shelf I find
A little volume, torn and thumbed,
    For comfort just designed.
I take my little Bible down
    And read its pages o'er
And when I part from it I find
    I'm stronger than before.
        Edgar A. Guest, 1991

I. MANUSCRIPT EVIDENCE FOR THE BIBLE

Can We Trust the Accuracy of Our Old Testament?

> "... and the Scriptures cannot be broken."
> (Jesus, John 10:35)

THE GREAT SYNAGOGUE

The Old Testament's 39 books are called "The Old Testament Canon." The word "canon" comes from an old English word, "kanon," that means to measure or that which has been measured and found up to the standard. Just how were the Old Testament books measured and by whom?

About 426 B.C. (the exact date is open to discussion) a group called "The Great Synagogue" came together to determine what was and was not Scripture. They met after they had just returned from the Babylonian Captivity. It was very important that Israel knew what was and was not Scripture. This group placed their approval on what today are our 39 Old Testament books. Since that time, the 39 books have been accepted by Jews, Jesus, the Apostles, and after Christ, by the church and Christians alike.

Who were these people of the Great Synagogue? They were Ezra, Nehemiah, Ezekiel, Daniel, and Zerubbabel, along with the Jewish priests and leaders who were the core of the Great Synagogue. Ezekiel and Daniel were probably not physically still present, but must have, in their old age, strongly expressed their opinions to the younger prophets who were the last biblical writers. Ezekiel and Daniel, who were captivity prophets, were giants of the Old Testament Prophets and their input was significant.

From the fifth century B.C. onward the Old Testament canon was settled and there were no other lists of Old Testament inspired books, accepted by the Jewish leaders, than the 39 the Jews honored and we have as our Old Testament today.

After the return of the Jews from the Babylonian Captivity the Temple was rebuilt and then the walls of Jerusalem were hurriedly re-built. It was therefore necessary for Israel to know, what were and what were not the inspired words of God.

There were many other books in existence, but which books were those endorsed by Isaiah, Daniel and the older prophets, and finally by Ezra and Nehemiah the younger prophets. The work was led by Ezra, Nehemiah, and Zerubbabel, the later Prophets, along with the Jewish leaders who endorsed what was and was not God's word.

THE BIBLE

We search the world for truth. We cull
The good, the true, the beautiful,
From graven stone and written scroll,
And all old flower-fields of the soul;
And, weary seekers of the best,
We come back laden from our quest,
To find that all the sages said
Is in the Book our mothers read.
John Greenleaf Whittier, 1807-1892

MOSES AND SEVENTY LEADERS

From Moses' time onward seventy leaders show up. Why? When Moses led the people out of Egypt, his father-in-law, Jethro, saw how overworked Moses was and how tired the people were waiting to have Moses pass judgment over critical matters that arose. He suggested to Moses that he should appoint seventy men to judge the people. (See Exodus 18:17-27 and Exodus 24:1 & 9.) This Moses did and a group of seventy leaders of Israel were appointed to judge Israel.

THE SEPTUAGINT

This group of seventy godly men, of Moses' time, judged the people. Seventy leaders show up at other times in the long history of Israel. For example, when Alexander the Great conquered the world, Greek became the language that was spoken around the Empire. (This was to be the language of the New Testament when it would be written two hundred years in the future.)

About 190 B.C., the Jews realized it would be helpful to have their Old Testament 39 books translated into Greek so everyone could read them, as many people could no longer read ancient Hebrew. Who oversaw this work? It was again a group of seventy. Their work was called the Septuagint (seventy). They chose to translate the same 39 books that the Great Synagogue had canonized.

A lot of the information surrounding the translation of the Septuagint may be an embellishment of what really happened, but we know for sure the work was approved by this group of seventy godly Hebrew scholars, thus the translation is called the Septuagint (Seventy).

What books did the Septuagint translators approve about 190 B.C.? As already said, they were the same 39 that the Great Synagogue had canonized. Those who question the age and authenticity of the book of Daniel have a problem because Daniel was one of the 39 canonical books approved by the

Great Synagogue and a part of the Septuagint. This was 190 years before Jesus was born. Daniel really did prophesy clear facts about the future and the coming of the Messiah.

THE SANHEDRIN

In the time of Jesus, we again find seventy leaders called the Sanhedrin. Their ancient history reaches back to the time of Moses and his setting up how Israel was to be governed.

It seems logical to suggest, then, that the Great Synagogue of Ezra and Nehemiah's day was made up of more than just the five men holding prophetic office. The three primary men (Ezra, Nehemiah, and Zerrubbabel) who led the Great Synagogue and placed their stamp of approval on our 39 Old Testament books were most likely many more than just the three. There was no doubt about what books comprised the Old Testament canon in the minds of Ezra and Nehemiah and from that point forward.

There are other times that these 39 books receive recognition along the way from the fifth century B.C. until the time of Jesus, when Jesus and His Apostles also placed their stamp of approval on these 39 books. There remains no question about what books should make up the Old Testament today.

THE DEAD SEA SCROLLS AND THE OLD TESTAMENT CANON

From the early 1950s until the mid-1960s A.D., the Dead Sea Scrolls were found and got their name, Dead Sea Scrolls, since they were found near the Dead Sea in Israel. They were mostly found in four caves at Qumran, a place that is near the northwest end of the Dead Sea.

The story of their finding is well known, but here is a brief review if some may not know it. A shepherd boy was hunting for some lost sheep and was standing on a ridge looking down and throwing rocks trying to find the lost ones. One of his rocks was thrown into an opening in the ridge and he heard the sound of pottery breaking. This Bedouin boy went in to explore the cave and found a large number of big pottery jars and inside them he discovered old leather manuscripts.

I have stood in the same place where the shepherd boy stood and looked into the cave where the majority of the scrolls were found.

The shepherd boy took some of these long pieces of leather out of the jars and took them home where they were hung up in their tent. They initially surmised that their value may have been in them being a fine quality of leather rather than for the old writing on them.

The boy's father took some of them into Jerusalem where he tried to sell them to antiquity dealers. He finally found a buyer in a man of the Syrian Orthodox Church named Metropolitan Samuel. Samuel bought them, recognizing them as probably very old biblical manuscripts.

Weeks later, Samuel was showing them to an American scholar, Dr. John C. Trevor, who requested permission to take one of the finer scrolls back to America for careful study. Back in America Dr. Trevor discovered that what he had was a very ancient copy of Isaiah, and after careful examination, he determined that it must have been written well before the birth of Christ. Eventually this scroll has been carefully dated 268 B.C.

When Samuel showed serious interest in buying more scrolls and the word got out that the scrolls were valuable, a hunting frenzy set in looking for more scrolls and eventually there were found about 900 of these ancient books. Primarily they were found in four caves near Qumran. A few partial documents were found near the synagogue at Masada at the scroll disposal site, and some others were found in other area caves near the original find.

According to the rules of the Scribes, when biblical manuscripts became so worn that they might not be clearly read, the Jewish scribes' practice was to make new clear copies and then bury or burn the old ones to assure that the older manuscript might not be misread and thus falsely transmit the word of God. This was the reason some manuscripts were buried outside the synagogue on Masada. It was a worn manuscript burial site.

In Christ's day there were three main religious/political parties in Israel—the Sadducees, the Pharisees, and the Essenes. The Pharisees and Sadducees pretty much ruled Jerusalem. The Essenes were a monastic group that had built a settlement, called Qumran, near the northwest end of the Dead Sea. This was to escape what they saw as the corrupting influence from the ruling parties in Jerusalem.

They had separated themselves from the other two groups in order to dedicate themselves to a study of scripture and to develop holiness in their lives. They saw that they had two choices: one was light, and the other darkness. To escape the infighting and not be drawn away from God, they led a monastic life in the desert. They were committed to the light and felt the leaders in Jerusalem and the whole world lay in darkness.

THE OLIVET DISCOURSE

Why did they hide their library? In Jesus' Olivet Discourse in Matthew 24, He predicted a terrible time of trouble that would come on Israel in the near future. This prediction saw its fulfillment when the Roman Generals Titus and Vespasian, father and son military leaders, came to subdue another rebellion of the Jews. This eventually led to the destruction of Herod's Temple, Jerusalem, Masada, and Gamla. At that time, A.D. 72, Israel was destroyed as a nation.

The Essenes, seeing this impending doom coming on them, wanted to preserve their most valuable possession—their fine library. They made large pottery bottles big enough to hold their scrolls, wrapped the scrolls in linen and sealed them in these jars and put them in caves nearby and covered over the entrances to hide them.

This explains how these old Bible books originated and survived.

They were incredibly important, since our oldest Hebrew handwritten Old Testament manuscripts are dated over 1,000 years later. The oldest complete Hebrew manuscript was called The Leningrad Codex, and was dated about A.D. 1017.

Many scholars and religious commentators have questioned the accuracy of our Old Testament books. One so-called modern "prophet," Joseph Smith, claimed that almost all of the Old and New Testaments books had been changed and edited by the Catholic Church during the Dark Ages. The Dead Sea Scrolls completely refuted those false claims. We now know what the Old Testament was that Jesus used and endorsed.

Of the about 900 scrolls found, 330 were of Old Testament books. There were eight copies of Genesis, ten copies of Exodus, and with 39 books in the Old Testament, this meant there were multiple copies of most books, some older and some a bit later. All were before A.D. 72 and the destruction of Jerusalem. Only one book was missing from the scrolls, the book of Esther.

METROPOLITAN SAMUEL

In the early spring of 1972, I was in Jerusalem and asked my friend Zach Jamjoum if he knew Metropolitan Samuel. He said he did and he knew where his office was. He gave me his phone number.

I called the office and was invited to come for a visit, which I did. I spent most of one morning visiting with Samuel. He showed me some of the scrolls still in his possession, and several scroll bottles that he still had. He confirmed that there were many Old Testament scrolls and there were hundreds of copies of the Old Testament books.

With the finding of the scrolls and this new information, it is now certain that our Old Testament has not been tampered with or revised. Dr. Trevor said, after examining the Isaiah scroll, which I have seen, that he was disappointed that after carefully comparing it with the oldest copy of Isaiah which was over

1,000 years later, the differences were so minor as to have no bearing on the meaning and so trivial as to only be of interest to biblical scholars.

Just think, we now have a copy of Isaiah written 268 years before Jesus was born. This book has 124 prophecies about Jesus in it that are quoted in our New Testament books. Add to this the hundreds of other prophecies of Jesus and we begin to comprehend just how valuable our Old Testament is to our Christian faith.

The conclusion is clear: the Old Testament is accurate and has been carefully preserved. Jesus' words have been confirmed, "... the Scriptures cannot be broken" (John 10:35).

Again, in the Sermon on the Mount Jesus said, "For truly I say to you, until heaven and earth pass away, not the smallest letter or stroke shall pass away from the Law, until all is accomplished" (Matthew 5:18).

In the Book of Revelation Jesus says, "And I will grant authority to my two witnesses (Old and New Testaments), and they will prophesy for twelve hundred and sixty days, clothed in sackcloth. These are the two olive trees and the two lamp stands that stand before the Lord of the earth. And if any one desires to harm them, fire proceeds out of their mouth and devours their enemies; and if anyone would desire to harm them in this manner he must be killed" (Revelation 11:1–5).

Without a doubt the Old Testament scriptures have survived with Divine protection. Their remarkable history and repeated documentation over the centuries removes all doubt as to their accuracy. They have the documentation of the Prophets, Jesus, the Apostles, and now about 2,000 years of testimony of the church of Christ. We can trust the Old Testament scriptures.

HOW FIRM A FOUNDATION

How firm a foundation, Ye saints of the Lord,
Is laid for your faith in His excellent Word!
What more can He say than to you He hath said,
To you who for refuge to Jesus have fled?

Fear not, I am with thee, O be not dismayed,
For I am thy God, and will still give thee aid;
I'll strengthen thee, help thee, and cause thee to Stand
Upheld by My gracious, omnipotent hand.

When through the deep waters I call thee to go,
The rivers of sorrow shall not overflow;
For I will be with thee thy trials to bless,
And sanctify to thee thy deepest distress.

When through fiery trials thy pathway shall lie,
My grace, all-sufficient, shall be their supply;
The flames shall not hurt thee, I only design
Thy dross to consume, and thy gold to refine.
George Keith

People trying to prove that the Bible has been revised and corrupted have an argument with the Great Synagogue, the Septuagint translators, and with Jesus and His Apostles. Whom would you trust to know the truth, these godly Jews, Jesus, the Apostles, or some modern-day false prophet or false teacher? Certainly Jesus was right, "the scriptures cannot be broken" (John 10:35).

Not all Christians, preachers, or church leaders know this information, so be patient and help them learn the truth. Certainly our goal should be to inform, not further divide the church. Are you looking for the perfect church?

THE PERFECT CHURCH

If you should find the perfect church
Without one fault or smear,
For goodness sake! Don't join that church
You'd spoil the atmosphere.

If you should find the perfect church
Where all anxieties cease
Then pass it by lest joining it
You mar the masterpiece.

If you should find the perfect church
Then don't you ever dare,
To tread upon such holy ground,
You'd be a misfit there.

But since no perfect church exists
Made of imperfect men,
Then let's cease looking for that church
And love the church we're in.

Of course it's not a perfect church,
That's simple to discern
But you and I and all of us
Could cause the tide to turn.

What fools we are to flee our post
In that unfruitful search,
To find at last where problems loom
God proudly builds His church.

So let's keep working in our church,
Until the resurrection.
And then we each will join that church,
Without an imperfection.
    Mavis Williams, Old Hickory Tennessee[3]

JOHN THE BAPTIST

With the coming of John the Baptist, the four hundred silent years (when there had been no Prophets) were completed and he ushered in the Christian age with his preaching, baptizing, and by placing his stamp of approval on Jesus when He came to John the Baptist for baptism in the Jordan River (Matthew 3:13–16).

SUMMARY

Although the above information is only a brief summary of what could be given, it is a concise history of how our Old Testament 39 books became what they are today. It is safe to say that from the time of Ezra and Nehemiah, and the Great Synagogue in the fifth century B.C., the Old Testament scriptures have remained essentially the same. We can trust the accuracy of these books of the Hebrew Prophets from Genesis to Malachi.

II. PROPHECY AS POSITIVE PROOF THAT JESUS IS THE MESSIAH

353 Prophecies about Jesus Are Quoted from the Old Testament in the New

*"Then he said to them, 'These are my words that I spoke to you while I was still with you, that **everything** written about me in the Law of Moses and the Prophets and the Psalms must be fulfilled'" (Luke 24:44).*

As we have already learned, every Old Testament book has an underlying theme—Jesus. Jesus Himself makes this claim:

"Then he said to them, 'These are my words that I spoke to you while I was still with you, that everything written about me in the Law of Moses and the Prophets and the Psalms must be fulfilled" (Luke 24:44).

These three divisions that Jesus cites—the Law, Prophets, and Psalms, were how the Jews divided their 39 Old Testament books. We now divide these same books into five sections: Law, History, Poetry, Major Prophets, and Minor Prophets. Jesus is saying that the whole Old Testament predicted His coming.

Jesus says that not only did He fulfill Old Testament prophecy about Him, but He further fulfilled "everything" written in the Law, Prophets, and Psalms about Him. That there are fulfilled prophecies is amazing, but for Him to match every last prophecy of the coming Messiah is an incredible claim. Is it true? Yes!

There are about 500 Jesus prophecies in our Old Testament, a few more or few less depending on how one understands them. This is astounding since no human can accurately predict the future. Some of these prophecies came as early as the time of the creation in Genesis 3:15.

A further astounding fact is that at least 353 of these prophecies of Jesus are quoted in the New Testament books. 101 are quoted from Psalms and 124 are quoted from Isaiah.

When I was a young man, our preacher, Earl Chambers, preached a sermon that consisted of only Old Testament quotations that predicted Jesus. When joined together they told the whole life of Jesus Christ. He used to preach this sermon quoting each Old Testament passage from memory.

Many different lists of these prophecies have been made by various scholars but the author's favorite list is given here. The Old Testament prophecy text is given on the left, what it says in the middle, and where it is quoted in the New Testament is shown on the right.[1]

353 PROPHECIES FULFILLED IN JESUS CHRIST

We can now know for sure that these are prophecies of Jesus due to their clarity and also because they are quoted as such by the inspired New Testament writers. It doesn't take much imagination to realize that Moses, David, Jeremiah, Isaiah, Zechariah, and all the other Prophets have had the future revealed to them by the one who is the Lord of history. They tell the story of the Messiah and His history, and it runs through the whole Old Testament beginning like a red cord, then red rope, and finally a red stream that is connected to the Messiah, who will come and bring salvation to the whole world.

There are many who have made lists of the Old Testament Jesus prophecies and some suggest that the total number is more than 500. Here we give a list of 353 Jesus prophecies because they are quoted as such by the New Testament writers. The list may miss some but still illustrates that Jesus'

---

[1] Several other lists are given in the Appendix

whole life was predicted by the Prophets. It is truly miraculous that Jesus says He has fulfilled "all" that the Prophets wrote about Him, not just some but every last prophecy (Luke 24:44).

Here, then, is the list. You may not want to read every text, but you can test the list to determine its accuracy.

"Lo, I come: in the volume of the book it is written of me" (Psalm 40:7).
"The testimony of Jesus is the spirit of prophecy" (Revelation 19:10).
"...all things must be fulfilled, which were written in the Law of Moses, and in the Prophets, and in the Psalms, concerning me"
(Jesus Christ, Luke 24:44).
"To Him give all the prophets witness" (Acts 10:43).

There are many additional prophecies about Jesus in the Old Testament, but the ones shown here are those quoted by the New Testament writers.

	PROPHECY	DESCRIPTION	FULFILLMENT
1.	Gen. 3:15	Seed of a woman (virgin birth)	Galatians 4:4–5, Matthew 1:18
2.	Gen. 3:15	He will bruise Satan's head	Hebrews 2:14, 1 John 3:8
3.	Gen. 3:15	Christ's heel would be bruised with nails on the cross	Matthew 27:35, Luke 24:39–40
4.	Gen. 5:24	The bodily ascension to heaven illustrated	Mark 16:19
5.	Gen. 9:26, 27	The God of Shem will be the Son of Shem	Luke 3:36
6.	Gen. 12:3	Seed of Abraham will bless all nations	Galatians 3:8, Acts 3:25, 26
7.	Gen. 12:7	The Promise made to Abraham's Seed	Galatians 3: 16
8.	Gen. 14:18	A priest after the order of Melchizedek	Hebrews 6:20
9.	Gen. 14:18	King of peace and righteousness	Hebrews 7:2
10.	Gen. 14:18	The Last Supper foreshadowed	Matthew 26:26-29
11.	Gen. 17:19	Seed of Isaac (Gen. 21:12)	Romans 9:7
12.	Gen. 22:8	The Lamb of God promised	John 1:29
13.	Gen. 22:18	As Isaac's seed, will bless all nations	Galatians 3: 16
14.	Gen. 26:2–5	The Seed of Isaac promised as the Redeemer	Hebrews 11:18
15.	Gen. 28:12	The Bridge to heaven	John 1:51
16.	Gen. 28:14	The Seed of Jacob	Luke 3:34

#	Reference	Description	Fulfillment
17.	Gen. 49:10	The time of His coming	Luke 2:1–7; Galatians 4:4
18.	Gen. 49:10	The Seed of Judah	Luke 3:33
19.	Gen. 49:10	Called Shiloh or one sent	John 17:3
20.	Gen. 49:10	Messiah to come before Judah lost identity	John 11:47-52
21.	Gen. 49:10	Unto Him shall the obedience of the people be	John 10:16
22.	Ex. 3:13-15	The Great "I AM"	John 4:26, 8:58
23.	Ex. 12:5	A Lamb without blemish	Hebrews 9:14; 1 Peter 1:19
24.	Ex. 12:13	The blood of the Lamb saves from wrath	Romans 5:8
25.	Ex. 12:21–27	Christ is our Passover	1 Corinthians 5:7
26.	Ex. 12:46	Not a bone of the Lamb to be broken	John 19:31–36
27.	Ex. 15:2	His exaltation predicted as Yeshua	Acts 7:55, 56
28.	Ex. 15:11	His Character—Holiness	Luke 1:35; Acts 4:27
29.	Ex. 17:6	The Spiritual Rock of Israel	1 Corinthians 10:4
30.	Ex. 33:19	His Character—Merciful	Luke 1:72
31.	Lev. 1:2–9	His sacrifice a sweet smelling savor unto God	Ephesians 5:2
32.	Lev. 14:11	The leper cleansed—Sign to priesthood	Luke 5:12–14; Acts 6:7
33.	Lev. 16:15-17	Prefigures Christ's once-for-all death	Hebrews 9:7–14
34.	Lev. 16:27	Suffering outside the Camp	Matthew 27:33; Heb. 13:11, 12
35.	Lev. 17:11	The Blood—the life of the flesh	Matthew 26:28; Mark 10:45
36.	Lev. 17:11	It is the blood that makes atonement	Rom. 3:23–24; 1 John 1:7
37.	Lev. 23:36-37	The Drink-offering: "If any man thirst"	John 7:37
38.	Num. 9:12	Not a bone of Him broken	John 19:31–36
39.	Num. 21:9	The serpent on a pole—Christ lifted up	John 3:14-18, 12:32
40.	Num. 24:17	Time: "I shall see Him, but not now."	John 1:14; Galatians 4:4
41.	Deut. 18:15	"This is of a truth that prophet."	John 6:14
42.	Deut. 18:15–16	"Had ye believed Moses, ye would believe me."	John 5:45–47
43.	Deut. 18:18	Sent by the Father to speak His word	John 8:28, 29
44.	Deut. 18:19	Whoever will not hear must bear his sin	Acts 3:22–23
45.	Deut. 21:23	Cursed is He that hangs on a tree	Galatians 3:10–13
46.	Joshua 5:14–15	The Captain of our salvation	Hebrews 2:10
47.	Ruth 4:4-10	Christ, our kinsman, has redeemed us	Ephesians 1:3–7
48.	1 Sam. 2:35	A Faithful Priest	Heb. 2:17, 3:1-3, 6, 7:24-25
49.	1 Sam. 2:10	Shall be an anointed King to the Lord	Mt. 28:18, John 12:15

50.	2 Sam. 7: 12	David's Seed	Matthew 1:1
51.	2 Sam. 7:13	His Kingdom is everlasting	2 Peter 1:11
52.	2 Sam. 7:14a	The Son of God	Luke 1:32, Romans 1 :3-4
53.	2 Sam. 7:16	David's house established forever	Luke 3:31; Rev. 22:16
54.	2 Ki. 2: 11	The bodily ascension to heaven illustrated	Luke 24:51
55.	1 Chr. 17:11	David's Seed	Matthew 1:1, 9:27
56.	1 Chr. 17:12-13	To reign on David's throne forever	Luke 1:32, 33
57.	1 Chr. 17:13	"I will be His Father, He ... my Son."	Hebrews 1:5
58.	Job 9:32-33	Mediator between man and God	1 Timothy 2:5
59.	Job 19:23-27	The resurrection predicted	John 5:24-29
60.	Psa. 2:1-3	The enmity of kings foreordained	Acts 4:25-28
61.	Psa. 2:2	To own the title, Anointed (Christ)	John 1:41, Acts 2:36
62.	Psa. 2:6	His Character—Holiness	John 8:46; Revelation 3:7
63.	Psa. 2:6	To own the title King	Matthew 2:2
64.	Psa. 2:7	Declared the Beloved Son	Matthew 3: 1 7, Romans 1:4
65.	Psa. 2:7, 8	The Crucifixion and Resurrection intimated	Acts 13:29-33
66.	Psa. 2:8, 9	Rule the nations with a rod of iron	Rev. 2:27, 12:5, 19:15
67.	Psa. 2:12	Life comes through faith in Him	John 20:31
68.	Psa. 8:2	The mouths of babes perfect His praise	Matthew 21:16
69.	Psa. 8:5, 6	His humiliation and exaltation	Hebrews 2:5-9
70.	Psa. 9:7-10	Judge the world in righteousness	Acts 17:31
71.	Psa. 16:10	Was not to see corruption	Acts 2:31, 13:35
72.	Psa. 16:9-11	Was to arise from the dead	John 20:9
73.	Psa. 17: 15	The resurrection predicted	Luke 24:6
74.	Psa. 18:2-3	The horn of salvation	Luke 1:69-71
75.	Psa. 22: 1	Forsaken because of sins of others	2 Corinthians 5:21
76.	Psa. 22:1	"My God, my God, why hast thou forsaken Me?"	Matthew 27:46
77.	Psa. 22:2	Darkness upon Calvary for three hours	Matthew 27:45
78.	Psa. 22:7	They shoot out the lip and shake the head	Matthew 27:39-44
79.	Psa. 22:8	"He trusted in God, let Him deliver Him"	Matthew 27:43
80.	Psa. 22:9-10	Born the Savior	Luke 2:7
81.	Psa. 22:12-13	They seek His death	John 19:6
82.	Psa. 22:14	His blood poured out when they pierced His side	John 19:34
83.	Psa. 22: 14, 15	Suffered agony on Calvary	Mark 15:34-37
84.	Psa. 22: 15	He thirsted	John 19:28
85.	Psa. 22:16	They pierced His hands and His feet	John 19:34, 37; 20:27
86.	Psa. 22:17, 18	Stripped Him before the stares of men	Luke 23:34, 35

#	Reference	Description	Fulfillment
87.	Psa. 22:18	They parted His garments	John 19:23, 24
88.	Psa. 22:20, 21	He committed Himself to God	Luke 23:46
89.	Psa. 22:20, 21	Satanic power bruising the Redeemer's heel	Hebrews 2:14
90.	Psa. 22:22	His resurrection declared	John 20:17
91.	Psa. 22:27-28	He shall be the governor of the nations	Colossians 1:16
92.	Psa. 22:31	"It is finished"	John 19:30, Heb. 10:10, 12, 14, 18
93.	Psa. 23:1	"I am the Good Shepherd"	John 10:11, 1 Peter 2:25
94.	Psa. 24:3	His exaltation predicted	Acts 1:11; Philippians 2:9
95.	Psa. 30:3	His resurrection predicted	Acts 2:32
96.	Psa. 31:5	"Into thy hands I commit My spirit"	Luke 23:46
97.	Psa. 31:11	His acquaintances fled from Him	Mark 14:50
98.	Psa. 31:13	They took counsel to put Him to death	Mt. 27:1, John 11:53
99.	Psa. 31:14, 15	"He trusted in God, let Him deliver him"	Matthew 27:43
100.	Psa. 34:20	Not a bone of Him broken	John 19:31-36
101.	Psa. 35:11	False witnesses rose up against Him	Matthew 26:59
102.	Psa. 35:19	He was hated without a cause	John 15:25
103.	Psa. 38:11	His friends stood afar off	Luke 23:49
104.	Psa. 38:12	Enemies try to entangle Him by craft	Mark 14:1, Mt. 22:15
105.	Psa. 38:12-13	Silent before His accusers	Matthew 27:12-14
106.	Psa. 38:20	He went about doing good	Acts 10:38
107.	Psa. 40:2-5	The joy of His resurrection predicted	John 20:20
108.	Psa. 40:6-8	His delight—the will of the Father	John 4:34, Heb. 10:5-10
109.	Psa. 40:9	He was to preach righteousness in Israel	Matthew 4:17
110.	Psa. 40:14	Confronted by adversaries in the Garden	John 18:4-6
111.	Psa. 41:9	Betrayed by a familiar friend	John 13:18
112.	Psa. 45:2	Words of grace come from His lips	John 1:17, Luke 4:22
113.	Psa. 45:6	To own the title, God or Elohim	Hebrews 1:8
114.	Psa. 45:7	A special anointing by the Holy Spirit	Mt. 3:16; Heb. 1:9
115.	Psa. 45:7, 8	Called the Christ (Messiah or Anointed)	Luke 2:11
116.	Psa. 45:17	His name remembered forever	Ephesians 1:20-21, Heb. 1:8
117.	Psa. 55:12-14	Betrayed by a friend, not an enemy	John 13:18
118.	Psa. 55:15	Unrepentant death of the betrayer	Matthew 27:3-5; Acts 1:16-19
119.	Psa. 68:18	To give gifts to men	Ephesians 4:7-16
120.	Psa. 68:18	Ascended into Heaven	Luke 24:51
121.	Psa. 69:4	Hated without a cause	John 15:25

#	Reference	Description	Fulfillment
122.	Psa. 69:8	A stranger to own brethren	John 1:11, 7:5
123.	Psa. 69:9	Zealous for the Lord's House	John 2:17
124.	Psa. 69:14–20	Messiah's anguish of soul before crucifixion	Matthew 26:36–45
125.	Psa. 69:20	"My soul is exceeding sorrowful."	Matthew 26:38
126.	Psa. 69:21	Given vinegar in thirst	Matthew 27:34
127.	Psa. 69:26	The Savior given and smitten by God	John 17:4; 18:11
128.	Psa. 72: 10, 11	Great persons were to visit Him	Matthew 2: 1–11
129.	Psa. 72:16	The corn of wheat to fall into the ground	John 12:24–25
130.	Psa. 72: 17	Belief on His name will produce offspring	John 1: 12, 13
131.	Psa. 72:17	All nations shall be blessed by Him	Galatians 3: 8
132.	Psa. 72: 17	All nations shall call Him blessed	John 12:13, Rev. 5:8–12
133.	Psa. 78:1–2	He would teach in parables	Matthew 13:34–35
134.	Psa. 78:2b	To speak the wisdom of God with authority	Matthew 7:29
135.	Psa. 80:17	The Man of God's right hand	Mark 14:61–62
136.	Psa. 88	The suffering and reproach of Calvary	Matthew 27:26-50
137.	Psa. 88:8	They stood afar off and watched	Luke 23:49
138.	Psa. 89:27	Firstborn	Colossians 1:15, 18
139.	Psa. 89:27	Emmanuel to be higher than earthly kings	Luke 1:32, 33
140.	Psa. 89:35–37	David's Seed, throne, kingdom endure forever	Luke 1:32, 33
141.	Psa. 89:36–37	His character—Faithfulness	Revelation 1:5, 19:11
142.	Psa. 90:2	He is from everlasting (Micah 5:2)	John 1:1
143.	Psa. 91:11, 12	Identified as Messianic; used to tempt Christ	Luke 4:10, 11
144.	Psa. 97:9	His exaltation predicted	Acts 1: 11; Ephesians 1:20
145.	Psa. 100:5	His character—goodness	Matthew 19:16, 17
146.	Psa. 102:1–11	The suffering and reproach of Calvary	John 19:16–30
147.	Psa. 102:25–27	Messiah is the Preexistent Son	Hebrews 1:10–12
148.	Psa. 109:25	Ridiculed	Matthew 27:39
149.	Psa. 110:1	Son of David	Matthew 22:42–43
150.	Psa. 110:1	To ascend to the right-hand of the Father	Mark 16:19
151.	Psa. 110:1	David's son called Lord	Matthew 22:44, 45
152.	Psa. 110:4	A priest after Melchizedek's order	Hebrews 6:20
153.	Psa. 112:4	His character—compassionate, gracious, et al	Matthew 9:36
154.	Psa. 118:17, 18	Messiah's resurrection assured	Luke 24:5–7; l Cor. 15:20
155.	Psa. 118:22, 23	The rejected stone is Head of the corner	Matthew 21:42, 43
156.	Psa. 118:26a	The Blessed One presented to Israel	Matthew 21:9
157.	Psa. 118:26b	To come while Temple standing	Matthew 21:12–15

#	Reference	Description	Fulfillment
158.	Psa. 132:11	The Seed of David (the fruit of His Body)	Luke 1:32, Acts 2:30
159.	Psa. 129:3	He was scourged	Matthew 27:26
160.	Psa. 138:1–6	The supremacy of David's Seed amazes six kings	Matthew 2:2–6
161.	Psa. 147:3, 6	The earthly ministry of Christ described	Luke 4:18
162.	Prov. 1:23	He will send the Spirit of God	John 16:7
163.	Prov. 8:23	Foreordained from everlasting	Rev. 13:8, 1 Pet 1:19–20
164.	Song 5:16	The altogether lovely One	John 1:17
165.	Isa. 2:3	He shall teach all nations	John 4:25
166.	Isa. 2:4	He shall judge among the nations	John 5:22
167.	Isa. 6:1	When Isaiah saw His glory	John 12:40–41
168.	Isa. 6:8	The One sent by God	John 12:38–45
169.	Isa. 6:9–10	Parables fall on deaf ears	Matthew 13:13–15
170.	Isa. 6:9–12	Blinded to Christ and deaf to His words	Acts 28:23–29
171.	Isa. 7: 14	To be born of a virgin	Luke 1:35
172.	Isa. 7: 14	To be Emmanuel—God with us	Matthew 1:18-23, 1 Tim. 3:16
173.	Isa. 8:8	Called Emmanuel	Matthew 28:20
174.	Isa. 8:14	A stone of stumbling, a rock of offense	l Peter 2:8
175.	Isa. 9:1, 2	His ministry to begin in Galilee	Matthew 4:12–17
176.	Isa. 9:6	A child born—humanity	Luke 1:31
177.	Isa. 9:6	A Son given—deity	Luke 1:32, John 1:14, 1 Tim. 3:16
178.	Isa. 9:6	Declared to be the Son of God with power	Romans 1:3, 4
179.	Isa. 9:6	The Wonderful One, Peleh	Luke 4:22
180.	Isa. 9:6	The Counselor, Yaatz	Matthew 13:54
181.	Isa. 9:6	The Mighty God, El Gibor	1 Cor. 1:24, Titus 2:3
182.	Isa. 9:6	The Everlasting Father, Avi Adth	John 8:58, 10:30
183.	Isa. 9:6	The Prince of Peace, Sar Shalom	John 16:33
184.	Isa. 9:7	To establish an everlasting kingdom	Luke 1:32–33
185.	Isa. 9:7	His Character—just	John 5:30
186.	Isa. 9:7	No end to his government, throne, and peace	Luke 1:32–33
187.	Isa. 11: 1	Called a Nazarene—the Branch, Natzar	Matthew 2:23
188.	Isa. 11:1	A rod out of Jesse—Son of Jesse	Luke 3:23, 32
189.	Isa. 11:2	Anointed One by the Spirit	Matthew 3:16, 17, Acts 10:38
190.	Isa. 11:2	His Character—Wisdom, Knowledge, et al	Colossians 2:3
191.	Isa. 11:3	He would know their thoughts	Luke 6:8, John 2:25
192.	Isa. 11:4	Judge in righteousness	Acts 17:31
193.	Isa. 11:4	Judges with the sword of His mouth	Rev. 2:16, 19:11, 15

#	Verse	Description	Reference
194.	Isa. 11:5	Character: Righteous & Faithful	Rev. 19:11
195.	Isa. 11:10	The Gentiles seek Him	John 12:18–21
196.	Isa. 12:2	Called Jesus—Yeshua	Matthew 1:21
197.	Isa. 22:22	The One given all authority to govern	Revelation 3:7
198.	Isa. 25:8	The Resurrection predicted	1 Corinthians 15:54
199.	Isa. 26:19	His power of Resurrection predicted	Matthew 27:50–54
200.	Isa. 28:16	The Messiah is the precious cornerstone	Acts 4:11, 12
201.	Isa. 28:16	The sure foundation	1 Corinthians 3:11, Mt. 16:18
202.	Isa. 29:13	He indicated hypocritical obedience to His Word	Matthew 15:7–9
203.	Isa. 29:14	The wise are confounded by the Word	1 Corinthians 1: 18-31
204.	Isa. 32:2	A refuge—a man shall be a hiding place	Matthew 23:37
205.	Isa. 35:4	He will come and save you	Matthew 1:21
206.	Isa. 35:5–6	To have a ministry of miracles	Matthew 11:2–6
207.	Isa. 40:3, 4	Preceded by forerunner	John 1:23
208.	Isa. 40:9	"Behold your God."	John 1:36; 19:14
209.	Isa. 40:10.	He will come to reward	Revelation 22: 12
210.	Isa. 40:11	A shepherd—compassionate life-giver	John 10:10–18
211.	Isa. 42:1–4	The Servant—as a faithful, patient redeemer	Matthew 12:18–21
212.	Isa. 42:2	Meek and lowly	Matthew 11:28–30
213.	Isa. 42:3	He brings hope for the hopeless	John 4
214.	Isa. 42:4	The nations shall wait on His teachings	John 12:20–26
215.	Isa. 42:6	The Light (salvation) of the Gentiles	Luke 2:32
216.	Isa. 42:1, 6	His is a worldwide compassion	Matthew 28: 19, 20
217.	Isa. 42:7	Blind eyes opened	John 9:25–38
218.	Isa. 43:11	He is the only Savior	Acts 4:12
219.	Isa. 44:3	He will send the Spirit of God	John 16:7, 13
220.	Isa. 45:21–25	He is Lord and Savior	Philippians 3:20, Titus 2:13
221.	Isa. 45:23	He will be the Judge	John 5:22; Romans 14:11
222.	Isa. 46:9, 10	Declares things not yet done	John 13:19
223.	Isa. 48:12	The First and the Last	John 1:30, Revelation 1:8, 17
224.	Isa. 48:16, 17	He came as a Teacher	John 3:2
225.	Isa. 49: 1	Called from the womb—His humanity	Matthew 1: 18
226.	Isa. 49:5	A Servant from the womb.	Luke 1:31, Philippians 2:7
227.	Isa. 49:6	He will restore Israel	Acts 3:19–21, 15:16–17
228.	Isa. 49:6	He is salvation for Israel	Luke 2:29-32
229.	Isa. 49:6	He is the light of the Gentiles	John 8: 12, Acts 13:47
230.	Isa. 49:6	He is salvation unto the ends of the earth	Acts 15:7–18

#	Verse	Description	Fulfillment
231.	Isa. 49:7	He is despised of the Nation	John 1:11, 8:48–49, 19:14–15
232.	Isa. 50:3	Heaven is clothed in black at His humiliation	Luke 23:44, 45
233.	Isa. 50:4	He is a learned counselor for the weary	Matthew 7:29, 11:28, 29
234.	Isa. 50:5	The Servant bound willingly to obedience	Matthew 26:39
235.	Isa. 50:6a	"I gave my back to the smiters."	Matthew 2 7:26
236.	Isa. 50:6b	He was smitten on the cheeks	Matthew 26:67
237.	Isa. 50:6c	He was spat upon	Matthew 27:30
238.	Isa. 52:7	Published good tidings upon mountains	Matthew 5:12, 15:29, 28:16
239.	Isa. 52:13	The Servant exalted	Acts 1:8-11; Eph. 1:19–22, Ph. 2:5–9
240.	Isa. 52:14	The Servant shockingly abused	Luke 18:31–34; Mt. 26:67, 68
241.	Isa. 52:15	Nations startled by message of the Servant	Luke 18:31–34; Mt. 26:67, 68
242.	Isa. 52:15	His blood shed sprinkles nations	Hebrews 9:13–14, Rev. 1:5
243.	Isa. 53:1	His people would not believe Him	John 12:37–38
244.	Isa. 53:2	Appearance of an ordinary man	Philippians 2:6–8
245.	Isa. 53:3a	Despised	Luke 4:28–29
246.	Isa. 53:3b	Rejected	Matthew 27:21–23
247.	Isa. 53:3c	Great sorrow and grief	Matthew 26:37–38, Luke 19:41; Heb. 4:15
248.	Isa. 53:3d	Men hide from being associated with Him	Mark 14:50–52
249.	Isa. 53:4a	He would have a healing ministry	Matthew 8:16–17
250.	Isa. 53:4b	Thought to be cursed by God	Matthew 26:66, 27:41–43
251.	Isa. 53:5a	Bears penalty for mankind's iniquities	2 Cor. 5:21, Heb. 2:9
252.	Isa. 53:5b	His sacrifice provides peace between man and God	Colossians 1:20
253.	Isa. 53:5c	His sacrifice would heal man of sin	1 Peter 2:24
254.	Isa. 53:6a	He would be the sin-bearer for all mankind	1 John 2:2, 4:10
255.	Isa. 53:6b	God's will that He bear sin for all mankind	Galatians 1:4
256.	Isa. 53:7a	Oppressed and afflicted	Matthew 27:27–31
257.	Isa. 53:7b	Silent before his accusers	Matthew 27:12–14
258.	Isa. 53:7c	Sacrificial lamb	John 1:29, 1 Peter 1:18–19
259.	Isa. 53:8a	Confined and persecuted	Matthew 26:47-27:31
260.	Isa. 53:8b	He would be judged	John 18:13–22
261.	Isa. 53:8c	Killed	Matthew 27:35

262.	Isa. 53:8d	Dies for the sins of the world	1 John 2:2
263.	Isa. 53:9a	Buried in a rich man's grave	Matthew 27:57
264.	Isa. 53:9b	Innocent and had done no violence	Luke 23:41, John 18:38
265.	Isa. 53:9c	No deceit in His mouth	1 Peter 2:22
266.	Isa. 53:10a	God's will that He die for mankind	John 18:11
267.	Isa. 53:10b	An offering for sin	Matthew 20:28, Galatians 3:13
268.	Isa. 53:10c	Resurrected and live forever	Romans 6:9
269.	Isa. 53:10d	He would prosper	John 17:1–5
270.	Isa. 53:11a	God fully satisfied with His suffering	John 12:27
271.	Isa. 53:11b	God's servant would justify man	Romans 5:8–9, 18–19
272.	Isa. 53:11c	The sin-bearer for all mankind	Hebrews 9:28
273.	Isa. 53:12a	Exalted by God because of His sacrifice	Matthew 28:18
274.	Isa. 53:12b	He would give up His life to save mankind	Luke 23:46
275.	Isa. 53:12c	Numbered with the transgressors	Mark 15:27–28
276.	Isa. 53:12d	Sin-bearer for all mankind	1 Peter 2:24
277.	Isa. 53:12e	Intercede to God on behalf of mankind	Luke 23:34, Rom. 8:34
278.	Isa. 55:3	Resurrected by God	Acts 13:34
279.	Isa. 55:4a	A witness	John 18:37
280.	Isa. 55:4b	He is a leader and commander	Hebrews 2:10
281.	Isa. 55:5	God would glorify Him	Acts 3:13
282.	Isa. 59:16a	Intercessor between man and God	Matthew 10:32
283.	Isa. 59:16b	He would come to provide salvation	John 6:40
284.	Isa. 59:20	He would come to Zion as their Redeemer	Luke 2:38
285.	Isa. 60:1–3	He would shew light to the Gentiles	Acts 26:23
286.	Isa. 61:1a	The Spirit of God upon Him	Matthew 3:16–17
287.	Isa. 61:1b	The Messiah would preach the good news	Luke 4:16–21
288.	Isa. 61:1c	Provide freedom from the bondage of sin	John 8:31–36
289.	Isa. 61:1–2a	Proclaim a period of grace	Galatians 4:4–5
290.	Jer. 23:5–6	Descendant of David	Luke 3:23–31
291.	Jer. 23:5–6	The Messiah would be both God and man	John 13:13, 1 Tim 3:16
292.	Jer. 31:22	Born of a virgin	Matthew 1:18–20
293.	Jer. 31:31	The Messiah would be the new covenant	Matthew 26:28
294.	Jer. 33:14–15	Descendant of David	Luke 3:23–31
295.	Eze.34:23–24	Descendant of David	Matthew 1:1
296.	Eze.37:24–25	Descendant of David	Luke 1:31–33
297.	Dan. 2:44–45	The Stone that shall break the kingdoms	Matthew 21:44
298.	Dan. 7: 13–14a	He would ascend into heaven	Acts 1:9–11

#	Verse	Description	Reference
299.	Dan. 7:13–14b	Highly exalted	Ephesians 1:20–22
300.	Dan. 7:13–14c	His dominion would be everlasting	Luke 1:31–33
301.	Dan. 9:24a	To make an end to sins	Galatians 1:3–5
302.	Dan. 9:24a	To make reconciliation for iniquity	Romans 5:10, 2 Cor. 5:18–21
303.	Dan. 9:24b	He would be holy	Luke 1:35
304.	Dan. 9:25	His announcement	John 12:12–13
305.	Dan. 9:26a	Cut off	Matthew 16:21, 21:38–39
306.	Dan. 9:26b	Die for the sins of the world	Hebrews 2:9
307.	Dan. 9:26c	Killed before the destruction of the temple	Matthew 27:50–51
308.	Dan. 10:5–6	Messiah in a glorified state	Revelation 1: 13–16
309.	Hos. 11:1	He would be called out of Egypt	Matthew 2:15
310.	Hos. 13:14	He would defeat death	Corinthians 15:55–57
311.	Joel 2:32	Offer salvation to all mankind	Romans 10:9–13
312.	Jonah 1:17	Death and resurrection of Christ	Matthew 12:40, 16:4
313.	Mic. 5:2a	Born in Bethlehem	Matthew 2: 1–6
314.	Mic. 5:2b	Ruler in Israel	Luke 1:33
315.	Mic. 5:2c	From everlasting	John 8:58
316.	Hag. 2:6–9	He would visit the second Temple	Luke 2:27–32
317.	Hag. 2:23	Descendant of Zerubbabel	Luke 2:27–32
318.	Zech. 3:8	God's servant	John 17:4
319.	Zech. 6:12–13	Priest and King	Hebrews 8:1
320.	Zech. 9:9a	Greeted with rejoicing in Jerusalem	Matthew 21:8–10
321.	Zech. 9:9b	Beheld as King	John 12:12–13
322.	Zech. 9:9c	The Messiah would be just	John 5:30
323.	Zech. 9:9d	The Messiah would bring salvation	Luke 19:10
324.	Zech. 9:9e	The Messiah would be humble	Matthew 11:29
325.	Zech. 9:9f	Presented to Jerusalem riding on a donkey	Matthew 21:6–9
326.	Zech. 10:4	The cornerstone	Ephesians 2:20
327.	Zech. 11:4–6a	At His coming, Israel to have unfit leaders	Matthew 23: 1–4
328.	Zech. 11:4–6b	Rejection causes God to remove His protection	Luke 19:41–44
329.	Zech. 11:4–6c	Rejected in favor of another king	John 19:13–15
330.	Zech. 11:7	Ministry to "poor," the believing remnant	Matthew 9:35–36
331.	Zech. 11:8a	Unbelief forces Messiah to reject them	Matthew 23:33
332.	Zech. 11:8b	Despised	Matthew 27:20
333.	Zech. 11:9	Stops ministering to those who rejected Him	Matthew 13:10–11
334.	Zech. 11:10–11a	Rejection causes God to remove protection	Luke 19:41–44

335.	Zech.11:10–11b	The Messiah would be God	John 14:7
336.	Zech. 11:12–13a	Betrayed for thirty pieces of silver	Matthew 26:14–15
337.	Zech. 11:12–13b	Rejected	Matthew 26:14–15
338.	Zech. 11:12–13c	Thirty pieces of silver cast in the house of the Lord	Matthew 27:3–5
339.	Zech. 11:12–13d	The Messiah would be God	John 12:45
340.	Zech. 12:10a	The Messiah's body would be pierced	John 19:34–37
341.	Zech. 12:10b	The Messiah would be both God and man	John 10:30
342.	Zech. 12:10c	The Messiah would be rejected	John 1:11
343.	Zech. 13:7a	God's will He die for mankind	John 18:11
344.	Zech. 13:7b	A violent death	Mark 14:27
345.	Zech. 13:7c	Both God and man	John 14:9
346.	Zech. 13:7d	Israel scattered as a result of rejecting Him	Matthew 26:31–56
347.	Zech. 14:4	He would return to the Mt. of Olives	Acts 1:11–12
348.	Mal. 3:1a	Messenger to prepare the way for Messiah	Mark 1:1–8
349.	Mal. 3:1b	Sudden appearance at the temple	Mark 11:15–16
350.	Mal. 3:1c	Messenger of the New Covenant	Luke 4:43
351.	Mal. 3:6	The God who changes not	Hebrews 13:8
352.	Mal. 4:5	Forerunner in spirit of Elijah	Mt. 3:1-3, 11:10–14, 17:11–13
353.	Mal. 4:6	Forerunner would turn many to righteousness	Luke 1:16–17

JESUS AS THE "I AM"

In addition to the many direct prophecies in the above list, consider as well that Jesus is a part of the eternal Godhead. Jesus claims to be the "I Am," which means that everywhere we find the word "Jehovah" in the Old Testament it is in reality a reference to Jesus also. This adds an additional 7,000 references to Jesus. The word Jehovah literally means "I Am."

Jesus spoke of Himself as the "I Am":

"So the Jews said to him, 'You are not yet fifty years old, and have you seen Abraham?' Jesus said to them, 'Truly, truly, I say to you, before Abraham was, I am.' So they picked up stones to throw at him, but Jesus hid himself and went out of the temple" (John 8:57–58).

The Jews were so distraught because they understood what Jesus was saying. Jesus was stating that He is the "I Am." In Exodus when Moses came to the burning bush and had a conversation with God, there God identifies Himself as the "I Am." "I Am" is a literal translation of the Hebrew word used in Exodus 3:14 where God says "I am who I am." The Hebrew word here is "JHVH" or Jehovah. This Hebrew word is the noun form of a verb that means "existence." God's name means that He is the source of all existence. He is the self-existent one, He is not dependent on anything else to exist.

Thereafter, God is referred to as Jehovah in the Old Testament about 7,000 times. Jesus clearly declares that He is the "I Am." On many other occasions Jesus speaks of Himself as "I am the good shepherd" or "I am the light" or "I am the truth" or "I am the water of life" and in reality, He is claiming to be Jehovah.

The conclusion to be drawn from this is that when the Old Testament refers to Jehovah, in fact it is a reference to Jesus.

This is further explained in the Gospel of John:

"In the beginning was the Word, and the Word was with God, and the Word was God. He was in the beginning with God. All things were made through him, and without him was not anything made that was made ... And the Word became flesh and dwelt among us, and we have seen his glory, glory as of the only Son from the Father, full of grace and truth ... No one has ever seen God; the only God, (Son) who is at the Father's side, he has made him known" (John 1:1–18).

Jesus says seven times in the Gospel of John that He is the "I Am."
"I Am the way." John 14:6
"I Am the truth." John 14:6
"I Am the light." John 8:12
"I Am the water of life." John 4:10; 14; 15 & 26
"I Am the vine." John 15:1 & 5
"I Am the life." John 14:6
"I Am the word." John 1:11–12 & 14

For a human to claim these things for themselves would be ludicrous. But when Jesus said these things, the Jews understood that Jesus was claiming to be God and the Jews believed He had committed a capital offense for which He should die. They tried to stone Him and eventually crucified Him. Jesus used the exact words of Exodus 3:14 where God gave His name and Jesus said that He was that one. This word is used about 7,000 times in the Old Testament scriptures.

Thus, Jesus is truly the theme that runs through the whole Old Testament. He can be shown to be a part of the theme of each book. He is predicted by about 500 prophecies; 353 of these prophecies are quoted by the New Testament writers, as documentation that Jesus is the Messiah and Savior of mankind. And finally, when we learn that Jesus and Jehovah are one, there are an additional 7,000 references to Jesus in our 39 books of the Old Testament.

Now just how did this happen when there are so many different authors, who wrote over so many years, and about so many differing subjects? How is it that the theme and core of the Bible is always Jesus? There cannot be any really serious answer other than that the Bible is a book inspired by God.

CONCERNING HIMSELF

Luke 24:25-27

Chosen men of God had spoken,	II Peter 1:20–21
O'er the years the Word had come,	Hebrews 1:1
Holy Writ cannot be broken,	John 10:35
In God's time—the Promised one.	Acts 13:23
Generations rising, falling,	Psalm 105:8
Waiting, hoping they might see,	Luke 2:25
Him, for whom their hearts were calling,	Romans 10:10
Lord of all eternity.	Psalm 90:2

Prophet after Moses' pattern,	Deuteronomy 18:15
Priest like Aaron, only pure,	Hebrews 4:14–16
King like David, but not earthen,	John 8:23
For this Kingdom shall endure.	Isaiah 9:7
Surely such a mighty ruler	Proverbs 23:11
Must with pomp and splendor come,	Isaiah 53:2
Few envisioned His appearing	Luke 19:43, 44
With a stable for His home.	Luke 2:12
Just as Scripture has foretold it	Isaiah 42:9
Lo, a Virgin shall conceive,	Isaiah 7:14
Child is born and Son is given,	Isaiah 9:6
Who would this report believe?	Isaiah 52:1
Grew in stature, rose in favor,	Luke 2:52
Hailed by Zachariah's son,	Luke 1:67–76
Lamb of God, repent and follow,	Luke 1:29
Signs and wonders being done.	Matthew 11:2–6
But beyond His life and teachings,	I Corinthians 15:3
To this end the Christ was born,	I John 3:8
That He give His life a ransom,	Matthew 20:28
Pardon, hope, for all who mourn.	Isaiah 61:1–3
To the cross our Lord was taken,	Matthew 27:31
In the tomb His body lay,	Matthew 27:57–60
Then in triumph He did waken,	Acts 1:3
Death to Life, O glorious day!	Revelation 1:18
For the cleansing blood, we're thankful,	I John 1:7

To a risen Christ we pray,   Timothy 2:5
Help us heed thy Great Commission,   Matthew 28:19, 20
Preach this Gospel every day.   Romans 1:16
    Shel Helsley

The marvel of how Jesus is woven throughout the Holy Bible boggles our minds. As with other marvelous things God has produced, we can only bow our hearts in faith, believing that Jesus is the Messiah.

PROPHETIC PREDICTIONS

Now let us turn our attention to prophetic predictions. Who can accurately predict the future? Wouldn't you love to have a stockbroker who could predict what is going to happen in the Market in a few days, weeks, or months?

In the 2016 United States presidential election the most skilled prognosticators, using all their modern technology, were completely wrong the night before the election was tabulated; so much for man's ability to predict the future.

It is true that we can see trends that lead to certain outcomes. We say to our children, "Touch that hot stove and you will get burned," or "Drive more carefully or you will get in a wreck." But we do not say, "Keep driving like that and you will have a wreck on Friday at 10 A.M. at Tenth and Broadway." No human knows that extent of the future. Yet, much more information about Jesus is given and about all of His life and work even to minute details. These predictions come hundreds and thousands of years in advance.

Before a couple marries, can they predict that they will have children, the gender of those children, their names, professions, their life's work, and how they will die? All of us know that such predictions cannot be made by humans. How then can we explain all of these predictions about Jesus and that He fulfilled not just a few of the 500, but every last one of them?

Josh McDowell wrote a very fine book, *Evidence That Demands a Verdict*.

In this book he discusses the laws of probability of prophecies of Jesus being fulfilled as they were. He cites a mathematician who says that if there were just seven Jesus prophecies fulfilled it would be a probability number of 10 to the 27th power. That would be 10 with twenty-seven zeros after it. He estimates that that number of silver dollars would cover the State of Texas two feet deep and there would be only one chance in that number of this happening. He suggests that a person be blindfolded and sent out to find the one and only dollar that was painted red. He must choose but one at random from all that covered Texas two feet deep. The fact is it could never happen. It is even less likely that these prophecies would be fulfilled accurately without supernatural intervention.

The mathematician went on to say if there were 27 prophecies fulfilled, that number probability would be 10 to the 157th power. That is 10 followed by 157 zeros. Again, how many silver dollars would that be? That number of silver dollars would overflow the known universe. [2]

Dr. Douglas Crane, when he heard McDowell's conclusion, said, "No that number is so large that it would be more than the molecules in the universe." The point is safely and conclusively made, there can be no doubt that prophecy proves that Jesus is the Christ, Messiah, and Savior of humanity. There can be no possibility of doubt. The only reason for unbelief is that one does not know the facts or that knowing the facts, their hearts are evil and they do not want to believe. It is not then a question of intelligence, but of integrity John 3:19.

The illustration set out above refers to only 27 prophecies, not 500. That small number produces a law of probability number so large as to be beyond our ability to comprehend it. What would the number be for 353, or 500, or 7,000? Inconceivable! This is absolutely positive proof Jesus is the Christ.

No human knows the future—only God does. But some may still doubt and suggest that Jesus was pretty clever and that He came and knew the Prophets and just did what they had predicted.

---

2   Josh McDowell, *Evidence that Demands a Verdict*, page 175

Think about that proposition for a moment. So Jesus decided to be born the right year, and chose to be born in the right town—Bethlehem? Jesus decided to be born of a virgin? Jesus decided to be raised in Nazareth? He decided to have the Jews and Romans kill him? This line of reasoning is filled with flaws. Why not just admit that Jesus has been proven to be the Messiah with irrefutable evidence? There can be no doubt.

CONSIDER SOME OF THESE ACTUAL PROPHECIES

Genesis

Here are a few of the Genesis prophecies of Jesus:

THE TREE IN PROPHECY

1. Genesis 3:1-7:

> "Now the serpent was more crafty than any other beast of the field that the LORD God had made. He said to the woman, 'Did God actually say, 'You shall not eat of any tree in the garden?' And the woman said to the serpent, 'We may eat of the fruit of the trees in the garden, but God said, 'You shall not eat of the fruit of the tree that is in the midst of the garden, neither shall you touch it, lest you die.' But the serpent said to the woman, 'You will not surely die. For God knows that when you eat of it your eyes will be opened, and you will be like God, knowing good and evil.' So when the woman saw that the tree was good for food, and that it was a delight to the eyes, and that the tree was to be desired to make one wise, she took of the fruit and ate, and she also gave some to her husband who was with her, and he ate. Then the eyes of both were opened,

and they knew that they were naked. And they sewed fig leaves together and made themselves loincloths."

The tree became the symbol of sin, disobedience and rebellion against God. This broke the personal relationship between God and them. Satan had taken the form of a serpent to tempt them to rebel against God. The serpent must have been more glorious then than they are today, in their condemned and fallen state. Serpents show up again in Moses' day to plague Israel when they rebelled and murmured against Moses and God.

These serpents and their work are talked about in Numbers 21:6–9. The people grumbled and God sent the serpents among them to bite them. Moses was told to set up a tree with a bronze serpent at the top. Those bitten by the serpents and who looked to the tree were saved; those who refused died. John 3:14 says that Jesus was lifted up on the tree and those who look to Him will be saved. Death came by a tree in the garden, life came by looking to a tree in Exodus, and at Calvary, solving the problem of the serpent.

AARON'S ROD THAT BUDDED

In Numbers 17:1–8, each of the tribes' leaders were to bring their rod or staff and God would indicate who was to be their High Priest. Aaron's dead staff grew overnight, bloomed, and bore almonds. It was a picture of the one who was dead and would live again to bear the fruit of righteousness.

THE BRANCH PROPHECIES

Then there are the "Natzar" passages in Isaiah and Jeremiah. Natzar is the Hebrew word for a verdant branch. The Messiah is predicted to come as the Natzar or Nazarene in Isaiah 4:2–6; 11:1–5; and shoot "Lphneo" or branch in Isaiah 53:1–2; 60:21; Jeremiah 23:5–6; 33:14–18; and Zechariah 3:8:10 and 6:12.

When Jesus came, he was raised in Nazareth, the city of verdant trees, and Nazareth remains so today. He grew up there and came to be called the

"Nazarene" in Matthew 2:23 and Acts 24:6. How did the Prophets know?

Jesus came to solve the problem of the fruit of the tree in Eden, was the fulfillment of Aaron's rod that budded, and is a Priest forever. Jesus came as the promised Natzar and Lphneo of Isaiah, Jeremiah, and Zechariah. Jesus did grow up in Nazareth and was called the Nazarene as He is the verdant branch.

Finally, Jesus combines all these trees: the sinful tree in Eden, the tree with the bronze serpent in the wilderness, Aaron's rod, the Natzar on the cross where He was crucified to solve humanity's problem that began in the Garden of Eden. He was crucified on a tree, a cross (John 19:17–18). Sin came because of the fruit of the tree and salvation came from the fruit of the tree at Calvary.

In summary, sin came from the tree of the Garden. Sin and the snake-bite's cure were found in looking to the tree in Moses' day. The Messiah was predicted in Aaron's (the Priest's) rod that budded. This was a symbol of the eternal Priest, Jesus, who lived after being dead. The Messiah, Jesus, would be a verdant tree. Sin began on a tree and its remedy came on a tree, the cross. Three days later the "Natzar" lived again. These two words speak of Jesus: "Branch" and "Shoot."

This kind of theme can be traced through the Old Testament with other illustrations. These prophecies of Jesus are subtle but indicate that the Author of the Bible knows history in advance.

2. Genesis 3:15:

> "And I will put enmity between you and the woman, and between your seed and her seed: He shall bruise you on the head, and you shall bruise him on the heel." (NASV).

The Septuagint translates the word seed as "sperma of woman." We all know that man, not woman, has sperm. Only once, in the virgin birth, does any woman have sperm without the aid of a man.

a) The seed of the woman speaks of the virgin birth. Women do not have seed, men do. There is only one case where women had seed—Mary, who gave birth to Jesus.

b) This seed would bruise Satan's head.

c) Christ's heel would be bruised with nails.

3. Genesis 12:3: the seed, (masculine singular in Hebrew), of Abraham would bless all nations. It would be only one descendant of Abraham who would bless everyone. Only in Jesus was this fulfilled, when Abraham's descendant became the savior of all mankind.

4. Genesis 14:17-20:

"After his (Abraham's) return from the defeat of Chedorlaomer and the kings who were with him, the king of Sodom went out to meet him at the Valley of Shaveh (that is, the King's Valley). And Melchizedek king of Salem brought out bread and wine. (He was priest of God Most High.) And he blessed him and said, 'Blessed be Abram by God Most High, Possessor of heaven and the earth; and Blessed be God Most High, who has delivered your enemies into your hand!' And Abram gave him a tenth of everything. "

This is a very interesting prophetic event. Here Melchizedek, a type of Christ, (Hebrews 6:20) meets Abram, a type of the Christian, (Galatians 3:29) and partakes of bread and wine, a type of communion, and Abram gave his tithe to Melchizedek. These are the very things we do in our modern church services today.

They met in the Valley of Shaveh, the King's Valley, which is the Kidron Valley, where later Jesus, the King of Kings, would pray in the garden, be arrested, tried, and crucified.

5. Genesis 22:1-8:

"After these things God tested Abraham and said to him 'Abraham!'

And he said, 'Here I am.' He said, 'Take your son, your only son Isaac, whom you love and go to the land of Moriah, and offer him there as a burnt offering on one of the mountains of which I shall tell you.' So Abraham rose early in the morning, saddled his donkey, and took two of his young men with him, and his son Isaac. And he cut the wood for the burnt offering and arose and went to the place of which God had told him. On the third day Abraham lifted up his eyes and saw the place from afar. Then Abraham said to his young men, 'Stay here with the donkey; I and the boy will go over there and worship and come again to you.' And Abraham took the wood of the burnt offering and laid it on Isaac his son. And he took in his hand the fire and the knife. So they went both of them together. And Isaac said to his father Abraham, 'My father!' And he said, 'Here I am my son,' He said, 'Behold, the fire and the wood, but where is the lamb for a burnt offering?' Abraham said, 'God will provide for himself the lamb for a burnt offering, my son.' So they went both of them together."

The parallels to Jesus are striking:

a) Offer your only son.

b) Go to the land of Moriah to a mountain God would show him. This is where Jesus would be crucified.

c) Two men were to be along, Jesus accompanied by two men.

d) Isaac was the same as dead for three days and nights in Abraham's mind.

e) Isaac carried the wood, Jesus carried His cross.

f) God would provide the lamb for sacrifice.

g) The lamb was caught in thorns and Jesus would wear a crown of thorns.

Often in the Old Testament the historical events are a picture of what would come later in the work and ministry of Jesus. These similarities are so striking that they cannot be happenstance.

When Jesus came and went about His life and work we understand better why God had asked such strange things of key people like Abraham. So many of these Old Testament events, like Abraham and Melchizedek's meeting in the King's Valley, are a picture of Christ and His church. Events like Abraham and Melchizedek with the bread, wine, and tithe, in the King's Valley are parallel to our worship today. These events would be repeated in the same place when Jesus would do His redeeming work. They are repeated all over the world each week today.

We have a clearer understanding of the reason that Abraham was asked to offer his only son, Isaac, as an offering, taking three days to travel sorrowfully from Hebron to what was to be Calvary. Why Isaac, who was the same as dead in Abraham's mind for three days and nights, who was spared by offering a lamb. It shows us how painful Jesus' death was for the Father, and that He was to be the Lamb of God, dying for the sins of the whole world.

We have observed just a few of the pictures and prophecies of Jesus found in the first book of the Bible. Many more could be shown. We now move on to two Bible books that are filled with Jesus prophecies: Psalms and Isaiah.

PSALMS 22 & 88

Psalm 22

The twenty-second Psalm of David may have had some meaning in David's own life, but much of it fits much more clearly in the life of Jesus, not David.

> "My God, my God, why have you forsaken me? Why are you so far from saving me, from the words of my groaning? Oh my God, I cry by day, but you do not answer, and by night, but I find no rest .... But I am a worm and not a man, scorned by mankind and despised by the people. All who see me mock me: they make mouths at me, they wag their heads; He trusts in the Lord, let him deliver him; Let him rescue him, for he delights in him!" (22:1–2, 6–8).

"Many bulls encompass me; strong bulls of Bashan surround me; they open wide their mouths at me, like a ravening and roaring lion. I am poured out like water, and all my bones are out of joint; my heart is like wax; it is melted within my breast; my strength is dried up like a potsherd, and my tongue sticks to my jaws; you lay me in the dust of death" (22:12–15).

"For dogs encompass me; a company of evildoers encircle me; they have pierced my hand and feet I can count all my bones—they stare and gloat over me; they divide my garments among them, and for my clothing they cast lots" (22:16–18).

"All the ends of the earth shall remember and turn to the Lord, and all the families of the nations shall worship before you ..." (22:27).

"... they shall come and proclaim his righteousness to a people yet unborn, that he has done it" (22:31).

Does the 22nd chapter of Psalms talk about David or Jesus?

a) Was David forsaken by God, both day and night?

b) When was King David ever publically displayed for mockery?

c) When were David's bones out of joint and his heart melted like wax?

d) When did anyone pierce his hands and feet?

e) When did anyone gamble over his clothes?

f) Did all the earth turn to the Lord because of David's suffering and everyone worship him?

g) Was David ever proclaimed as the savior to people yet unborn?

This Psalm is a prophecy about Jesus, His crucifixion and redeeming work among mankind. The real question is how did David know all of these things would happen to his descendant, Jesus? The answer to this question can only be by inspiration of God.

Psalm 88

Psalm 88 is clearly about Jesus and not about its authors, the sons of Korah. A little background may be helpful for those who have never had the chance to go into the house of the High Priest Caiaphas.

After Jesus was arrested and taken from Gethsemane, He ended up spending the night in Caiaphas' house. This house has been excavated and it is possible to walk from Gethsemane up the road and steps to the house.

It was a grand house, as would be expected of the home of the High Priest. One rather shocking feature of this house is that in the basement there is a dungeon with entry through a hole in the ceiling. A prisoner would be dropped or lowered into the cell below. There was no chance of escape.

In this dungeon Jesus spent at least part or most of the night when He appeared to be judged by the priests and High Priest (Matthew 26:57—27:1-2). Here Jesus was spat upon and slapped about and then placed for safe keeping in the pit below the High Priest's house until the morning, when He was bound and led away for another trial.

We now have the setting for this Psalm of Korah. There is no other known historical event that has happened as described in this Psalm that fulfills these awful words except a well-known event in the final hours of Jesus' life.

> "O LORD, God of my salvation; I cry out day and night before you. Let my prayer come before you; Incline your ear to my cry! For my soul is full of troubles, and my life draws near to Sheol. I am counted among those who go down to the pit; I am a man who has no strength, like one set loose among the dead, like the slain that lie in the grave, like those whom you remember no more, for they are cut off from your hand. You have put me in the depths of the pit, in the regions dark and deep. Your wrath lies heavy upon me, and you overwhelm me with all your waves" (88:1–7).

> "You have caused my companions to shun me; you have made me a horror to them. I am shut in so that I cannot escape; my eye grows

dim through sorrow. Every day I call upon you, O LORD; I spread out my hands to you. Do you work wonders for the dead? Do the departed rise up to praise you? Is your steadfast love declared in the grave, or your faithfulness in Abaddon? Are your wonders known in the darkness, or your righteousness in the land of forgetfulness?" (88:8–12).

"But I, O LORD, cry to you; in the morning my prayer comes before you. O LORD, why do you cast my soul away? Why do you hide your face from me? Afflicted and close to death from my youth up, I suffer your terrors; I am helpless, your wrath has swept over me: your dreadful assaults destroy me. They surround me like a flood all day long; they close in on me together. You have caused my beloved and my friend to shun me; my companions have become darkness" (88:13–18).

a) Jesus cries out day and night.

b) He is thrown down into the pit.

c) The pit is like a grave and He has no strength left in Him.

d) It is totally dark and deep.

e) He is experiencing God's wrath.

f) His friends and companions have shunned and deserted Him.

g) God has shunned and turned away from Him.

Can you imagine what Jesus was going through that night that He spent in the dungeon below Caiaphas' house? I find it impossible to go down into this pit and then read this Psalm without crying and sharing the anguish Jesus experienced in this awful place.

How did Korah and the Choir that sang this awful dirge know about these terrible events to come to Jesus so many years later? The answer is clear—by inspiration of God.

SPEAKING TO AND HEARING GOD

Dear Lord, my heart would thankful be
When in my prayer I speak to Thee;
Dear Lord, my heart would thankful be
When in Thy Book, You speak to me.
I speak in prayer; Thou hearest me
Thy Word is mine; there I hear Thee.
Robert Pattison

ISAIAH 7:14, 9:6–7; 52—53

With 124 prophecies about Jesus quoted in the New Testament from the Old Testament book of Isaiah, it is the richest source of Jesus prophecies in the entire Old Testament. Some are so clear it seems the writer must have been an eye-witness to the events. Yet we have proof that these are in fact prophecies. We now have the Dead Sea Scroll book of Isaiah written 268 B.C., and also the Septuagint Greek translation which was made about 190 B.C. We must look for other options to explain these clear prophecies made so many years before the events.

The Neo-orthodox scholars of Germany and France have tried to question the antiquity of Isaiah since they could not accept the doctrine of miracles or inspiration. At the time they wrote, they did not have the Dead Sea Scrolls. Their efforts to explain away the antiquity of this marvelous book have failed miserably. Yes, we now know without doubt that Isaiah had to have been inspired of God to write as he did about so many things in Jesus' life. Space does not permit more than a brief look at a few of these prophecies.

Isaiah 7:14

"Therefore the Lord himself will give you a sign. Behold, the virgin shall conceive and bear a son, and shall call his name Immanuel."

a) This was to be a sign from the Lord, something remarkable and spectacular.

b) A virgin shall conceive, yes, the word means a young woman that has never had sexual relations with anyone.

c) She is to not only have a child, but a male child.

d) His name would be Immanuel. This word means God with us.

This reminds us again of the prophecy of Genesis 3:15, the seed of the woman. There is only one such event in all of history—it is when the virgin Mary gave birth to Immanuel, God with us, Jesus.

Isaiah 9:6–7

> "For to us a child is born, to us a son is given; and the government shall be upon his shoulders, and his name shall be called Wonderful Counselor, Mighty God, Everlasting Father, Prince of Peace. Of the increase of his government and of peace there will be no end, on the throne of David and over his kingdom, to establish it and to uphold it with justice and with righteousness from this time forth and forevermore. The zeal of the Lord of hosts will do this."

These prophecies were fulfilled in Jesus Christ, the Messiah, the Savior of humanity. Here is the list:

a) He was to be a human child, a son.

b) He would be the head of a government that would rest upon His shoulders.

c) His names are reserved only for God. These names are; Wonderful Counselor, Mighty God, Everlasting Father, Prince of Peace. Has there ever been any other child born that could wear these names?

d) His kingdom would never end.

e) He would be a descendant of David and would rule on his throne and over his kingdom.

f) This would be a kingdom founded on righteousness and last forever.

g) God will guarantee that these things will happen, by his zeal.

These prophecies are astounding, and documentation that someone like Jesus would come, and come He did. No one else has ever even come close in matching these predictions.

Isaiah 52—53

While visiting with a Jewish Rabbi, I asked him what his view of Isaiah chapter 52 and 53 were. He thought for a few minutes and replied, "You are talking about the parable of the suffering servant, aren't you; it is puzzling to me just what that means."

I asked, "Have you ever considered that it might be talking about Jesus Christ?" He thought for a few moments and said, "Well, I have been told that but haven't come to accept it."

Our purpose is to only take a brief look at this scripture and then make a few comments. The question is, if this is not talking about Jesus, who then is it talking about?

> "Behold, my servant shall act wisely; he shall be high and lifted up, and shall be exalted. As many were astonished at you—his appearance was so marred, beyond human semblance, and his form beyond that of the children of mankind—so shall he sprinkle many nations; kings shall shut their mouths because of him; for that which has not been told them they see, and that which they have not heard they understand" (Isaiah 52:13–15).

a) This person would act wisely.

b) His appearance marred beyond recognition.

c) He would sprinkle many nations with his blessings.

d) Kings would become mute because of Him.

"Who has believed what he has heard from us? And to whom has the arm of the LORD been revealed? For he grew up before him like a young plant, and like a root out of dry ground; he had no form or majesty that we should look at him, and no beauty that we should desire him. He was despised and rejected by men, a man of sorrows, and acquainted with grief, and as one from whom men hide their faces, he was despised and we esteemed him not" (53:1–3).

a) Grew up as a tender plant out of dry ground.

b) Was not handsome, nor had majesty.

c) He was despised and rejected by people.

d) A sorrowful man.

e) Acquainted with grief.

f) He was not esteemed while He lived.

"Surely he has borne our griefs and carried our sorrows; yet we esteemed him stricken, smitten by God, and afflicted. But he was pierced for our transgressions, he was crushed for our iniquities; upon him was the chastisement that brought us peace, and with his wounds we are healed. All we like sheep have gone astray; we have turned—everyone—to his own way; and the LORD has laid on him the iniquity of us all" (53:4–6).

a) He bore our griefs and sorrows.

b) People thought Him stricken and smitten by God.

c) He was pierced for our sins and transgressions.

d) Our sins were placed on Him.

e) By His wounds we are healed.

f) The LORD laid all our iniquities on Him.

"He was oppressed, and he was afflicted, yet he opened not his mouth; like a lamb that is led to the slaughter, and like a sheep that before its shearers is silent, so he opened not his mouth. By oppression and judgment he was taken away; and as for his generation, who considered that he was cut off out of the land of the living, stricken for the transgression of my people? And they made his grave with the wicked and with a rich man in his death, although he had done no violence, and there was no deceit in his mouth" (53:-9).

a) With incredible suffering He remained silent.

b) He was condemned by oppression and lies.

c) His generation was cut off.

d) He was stricken for people's sins.

e) He would be buried in a sinful rich man's grave.

f) He had done nothing wrong yet was condemned for our sins.

"Yet it was the will of the LORD to crush him; he has put him to grief; when his soul makes an offering for guilt, he shall see his offspring; he shall prolong his days; the will of the LORD shall prosper in his hand. Out of the anguish of his soul he shall see and be satisfied; by his knowledge shall the righteous one, my servant, make many to be accounted righteous, and he shall bear their iniquities. Therefore I will divide him a portion with the many (great) and he shall divide the spoil with the strong, because he poured out his soul to death and was numbered with the transgressors; yet he bore the sin of many, and makes intercession for the transgressors" (Isaiah 53:10–12).

a) He would be crushed and put to grief as an offering for our guilt.

b) God would be satisfied by His suffering and He would make us sinners righteous.

c) He would be killed among transgressors.

d) He bore the sins of the world and prayed for us transgressors.

How could Isaiah have such a clear picture of Jesus when he wrote these words in the seventh century before Christ?

Here is a review of a few things Isaiah tells us about Jesus:

a) He would act wisely and be lifted high (52:13).

b) He would be marred more than any other human (v 14).

c) He would bring salvation to many nations (v 15).

d) He was not to be handsome, but despised and rejected (53:2).

e) He would bear our griefs and sorrows (v 4).

f) He would be smitten and pierced for our transgressions (v 5).

g) God laid all our iniquities on Him (v 6).

h) When afflicted he remained silent and was led to slaughter like a lamb (v 7).

i) He would be buried in a rich man's grave (v 9).

j) His soul was offered for our guilt (v 10).

k) The anguish of His soul purchased our salvation (v 11).

l) He would bring many to righteousness and bear their iniquities (v 12).

m) He would be slain among the transgressors, thieves, and bear the sins of many (v 12).

A person has only to be generally knowledgeable of the life of Jesus Christ to recognize that Isaiah has captured who and what Jesus was from childhood through His life and his death.

It is passages like these that have earned Isaiah the description of being the Old Testament gospel. These prophecies and the rest of this great book have earned it recognition as the prince of all literature. With its 124 prophecies about Jesus being quoted by the New Testament writers, it holds the record of having the most of any other Old Testament book. The New Testament writers have placed their endorsement upon Isaiah.

Our purpose is not to examine all of the prophecies of Isaiah or of the Old Testament but to give a brief overview that hopefully will not be too tedious for the novice student of scripture. This subject does deserve a much more extensive examination.

ETERNAL GOD WHOSE POWER UPHOLDS

Eternal God, whose power upholds
Both flower and flaming star,
To whom there is no here nor there,
No time, no near nor far,
No alien race, no foreign shore,
No child unsought, unknown,
O, send us forth, Thy Prophets true,
To make all lands Thine own!

O God of love, whose spirit wakes
In every human breast,
Whom love, and love alone, can know,
In whom all hearts find rest,
Help us to spread Thy gracious reign
Till greed and hate shall cease,
And kindness dwell in human hearts,
And all the earth find peace!

O God of truth, whom science seeks
And reverent souls adore,
Who lightest every earnest mind
Of every clime and shore,
Dispel the gloom of error's night,

Of ignorance and of fear,
Until true wisdom from above
Shall make life's pathway clear!

O God of beauty, oft revealed
In dreams of human art,
In speech that flows to melody,
In holiness of heart;
Teach us to ban all ugliness
That blinds our eyes to Thee,
Till all shall know the loveliness
Of lives made fair and free.

O God of righteousness and grace,
Seen in the Christ, Thy Son,
Whose life and earth reveal Thy face,
By whom Thy will was done,
Inspire Thy heralds of good news
To live Thy life divine,
Till Christ is formed in all mankind
And every land is Thine!
              Henry Hallam Tweedy

Daniel 9

The book of Daniel has many remarkable prophecies about world history and about Jesus and His kingdom. In chapter 2:31-45, Daniel interprets Nebuchadnezzar's dream of the statue. Daniel explains that the statue of gold, silver, bronze, iron, and clay are four kingdoms: Babylon, Medo-Persia, Greece, and Rome. Daniel explains that in the days of the Roman Empire, God would set up an everlasting kingdom.

    This remarkable prophecy is repeated in a different way with the four kingdoms pictured as a lion, bear, leopard, and the fourth beast that was terrifying and had huge iron teeth to devour the other kingdoms (Daniel 7:1–8).

But the most remarkable prophecy in Daniel is found in chapter 9. This is the prophecy of seventy weeks.

> "Seventy weeks are decreed about your people and your holy city, to finish the transgression, to put an end to sin, and to atone for iniquity, to bring in everlasting righteousness, to seal both vision and prophet, and to anoint a most holy place. Know therefore and understand that from the going out of the word to restore and build Jerusalem to the coming of an anointed one a prince, there shall be seven weeks. Then for sixty-two weeks it shall be built again with squares and moat, but in a troubled time. And after the sixty-two weeks, an anointed one shall be cut off and shall have nothing. And the people of the prince who is to come shall destroy the city and the sanctuary. Its end shall come with a flood, and to the end there shall be war. Desolations are decreed. And he shall make a strong covenant with many for one week, and for half of the week he shall put an end to sacrifice and offering. And on the wing of abomination shall come one who makes desolate, until the decreed end is poured out on the desolator" (Daniel 9:24–27).

Here is a summary of what Daniel tells us. His prophecy came at the end of the Babylonian Captivity:

> a) Prophecy uses symbolic language. This language has been used for events now past, fulfilled, and the interpretation is now clear. One example of this symbolic language is what is called "the day year" symbolism. Here are a few examples to illustrate the use of this day year idea. He says there would be 70 weeks. (Often in Bible prophecy a prophetic day equals a year in fulfillment.) We learn from Ezekiel 4:4 that each day that Ezekiel was to lie on his side represented a year. For Ezekiel, 390 days represented 390 years. This same reasoning is found in Numbers 14:34, there 40 days represented 40 years. Also in Revelation 11:3 & 9, 1,260 days represent 1,260 years. The day for a year concept also works exactly

here in Daniel chapter nine as well.

b) The beginning of the 470 (70 weeks) years was to be marked by the decree to restore and rebuild the Temple and Jerusalem. We know that date to be 457 B.C.

c) Sixty-two weeks plus seven more equal 69 weeks or 483 years. From 457 B.C., adding 483 years takes us to A.D. 26. (This misses the time of the beginning of Jesus' ministry by being four years too early. An examination of the years of history one will find that the Romans made a four-year mistake in our calendar. This means that the actual time would have been A.D. 30.) This is when the "anointed one, the prince" or Jesus would began His ministry.

d) The prince was to be cut off in the midst of the seventieth week or 486 years, which would have been A.D. 33, the year Jesus was crucified.

e) Daniel had predicted the exact year when Jesus' ministry was to begin and the very year He was to be crucified.

f) Daniel says these events would bring an end to the Law of Moses and bring in eternal salvation.

Here is the math:

The prophecy	70 weeks, 490 years
The edict to build was	457 B.C.
70 weeks minus 7 equals	483
457 minus 483 years sum is	A.D. 26
Roman mistake in calendar	4 years
Date when prince began his work	A.D. 30
To be cut off in midst of week, crucified	A.D. 33
Final desolation to come	A.D. 72
by Roman Generals Titus & Vespasian	

When I was a young preacher, and had first discovered this prophecy, and without the aid of the many modern resources that are available today, I was confused and spent days trying to figure this out. The main issue was the four-year mistake the Romans had made with the calendar. After days of research I learned of the Roman calendar mistake and that made this all work out exactly as predicted by Daniel.

The end result of this study was to see this remarkable prophecy in which Daniel predicts the exact year that Jesus would begin His ministry and would be crucified. How did Daniel know this more than a half a millennium before it happened?

When the neo-orthodox scholars realized what Daniel had predicted, they did not believe that it was possible. They then tried to prove that Daniel had been written after the events, since they did not believe in miracles, prophecy, or inspiration.

Today we have proof that Daniel was written well in advance of the birth of Christ since it was in the 39 books approved by the Great Synagogue and also found in the Septuagint, made 190 years before Jesus' birth.

THE BOOK OF BOOKS

Within this ample volume lies
The mystery of mysteries.
Happiest they of human race
To whom their God has given grace
To read, to fear, to hope, to pray,
To lift the latch, to force the way;
But better had they ne'er been born
Than read to doubt or read to scorn.
      Sir Walter Scott, 1771–1832

If you wish a more thorough study of Jesus prophecies in Daniel you can consult the list of 353 Jesus prophecies found in the Old Testament. This list of prophecies is given earlier in this book.

Micah 5:2–4

Micah lived from 749 to 697 B.C. This means that he wrote in the eighth century before Christ. Can you imagine trying to predict what will happen over seven hundred years from now? Micah makes several predictions that relate to the coming Messiah, but we will only look at two of the passages.

"But you, O Bethlehem Ephrathah, who are too little to be among the clans of Judah, from you shall come forth for me one who is to be ruler in Israel, whose coming forth is from of old from ancient days. Therefore he shall give them up until the time when she who is in labor has given birth; then the rest of his brothers shall return to the people of Israel. And he shall stand and shepherd his flock in the strength of the LORD, in the majesty of the name of the LORD his God. And they shall dwell secure, for now he shall be great to the ends of the earth. And he shall be their peace" (Micah 5:2–4).

    a) A ruler is to be born in Bethlehem.

    b) This child had existed from ancient days.

    c) There would be other children born to His mother later.

    d) He will shepherd the people.

    e) He would work in the strength and majesty of Jehovah.

    f) He will be great to the ends of the earth.

    g) And He would be our peace.

How could Micah know such remarkable things about Jesus? It was by the inspiration of the Holy Spirit. He also predicts a world-wide kingdom in Micah 4:1–2.

Zechariah 12—14

In the late sixth century before Christ, Zechariah wrote of the restoration of Jerusalem, and his predictions are told in eight visions. He writes to offer encouragement to rebuild the temple and he also predicts the coming of Christ.

Zechariah is filled with Jesus prophecies five hundred years before Jesus was born. We will only look at a few from the twelfth through fourteenth chapters. The message Zechariah brings is so clear it is like he is an onlooker to the actual events that would eventually happen. But, no, he writes from half a thousand years before.

> "And the LORD will give salvation to the tents of Judah first, that the glory of the house of David and glory of the inhabitants of Jerusalem may not surpass that of Judah. On that day the LORD will protect the inhabitants of Jerusalem, so that the feeblest among them on that day shall be like David, and the house of David shall be like God" (Zechariah 12:7–8).

> a) Judah would be the first to hear—not Jerusalem, as Bethlehem was in Judah and Jerusalem in Benjamin.

> b) Something very special will happen to the house of David.

> c) David's house shall be like God.

> "And I will pour out on the house of David and the inhabitants of Jerusalem a spirit of grace and pleas for mercy, so that, when they look on me, on him whom they have pierced, they shall mourn for him, as one mourns for an only child, and weep bitterly over him, as one weeps over a firstborn. On that day the mourning in Jerusalem will be as great as the mourning for Hadadrimon in the plain of Megiddo. The land shall mourn, each family by itself: the family of the house of David by itself, ..." (Zechariah 12:10–12).

> a) Something is going to happen in Jerusalem that will bring grace and mercy to the nations.

> b) They will look on someone from the house of David who has been pierced.

c) This is to be an only child, the firstborn.

d) There would be great mourning, especially the house of David would mourn.

"On that day there shall be a fountain opened for the house of David and the inhabitants of Jerusalem, to cleanse them from sin and uncleanness. And on that day, declares the LORD of hosts, I will cut off the name of the idols from the land, so that they shall be remembered no more. And also I will remove from the land the prophets and the spirit of uncleanness. And if anyone again prophesies, his father and mother who bore him will say to him, 'You shall not live, for you speak lies in the name of the LORD.' And his father and mother who bore him shall pierce him through when he prophesies ... Awake, O sword, against my shepherd against the man who stands next to me, declares the LORD of hosts. Strike the shepherd, and the sheep will be scattered; I will turn my hand against the little ones" (Zechariah 13:1–7).

a) A fountain will be opened in Jerusalem for sin and uncleanness.

b) Idolatry would cease among the Jewish people.

c) After the coming of Christ prophets and prophecy would cease.

d) Anyone who claims to be a prophet of God after that is a liar and to be killed.

e) A sword would come against the shepherd who is the colleague of Jehovah.

f) The shepherd would be stricken and His followers would be scattered.

"On that day living waters shall flow out from Jerusalem, half of them to the eastern sea and half of them to the western sea. It shall continue in summer as in winter. And the LORD will be king over all the earth. On that day the LORD will be one and his name one" (Zechariah 14:8–9).

a) Water, a symbol of blessings, will flow east and west from Jerusalem.

b) Jehovah, Jesus, will be king over all the earth, and His kingdom would be universal.

c) Jehovah would be united and His name one.

We can trust that these are Jesus prophecies due to their clarity and also because they are quoted as such by the New Testament writers. It doesn't take much imagination to understand that Zechariah predicts the restoration of Jerusalem which would result in the sacrifice for sin to cleanse people everywhere. This was fulfilled by the death of Jesus from which the whole world would receive grace and salvation.

The whole Old Testament sets the stage for the life and work of Jesus Christ. The prophecies are undeniable proof of whom and what Jesus was. These prophecies in themselves are positive and irrefutable proof that Jesus is the Messiah, but these prophecies are not the end of the story. The best and most positive proof of who Jesus was and is will be covered next: the resurrection.

III. THE RESURRECTION: PROOF OF JESUS AS MESSIAH

I CORINTHIANS 15

The resurrection of Jesus Christ may just be the most proven event in all of ancient human history. We will now look at some of these proofs that we have today.

If the resurrection can be proven, and it can, then it should be of primary interest to every human as we are all, in fact, terminal. For someone to teach there is life beyond the grave, and then to prove it by their resurrection, returning to life after having been dead three days. Should not this information attract all of our attention?

If Jesus does not have the answer for life beyond the grave, then who else in all of history does? If He does have the answer to humanity's greatest problem, what could be of greater importance? But if the resurrection is not true, this world is a pitiful tragedy. But the resurrection is true—the evidence for it is overwhelming and conclusive.

THE WITNESSES TO THE RESURRECTION

The Apostle Paul gives a brief summary of the eyewitnesses to the resurrection in I Corinthians 15.

"Now I would remind you, brothers, of the gospel I preached to you, which you received, in which you stand, and by which you are being saved, if you hold fast to the word I preached to you—unless you believed in vain."

"For I delivered to you as of first importance what I also received: that Christ died for our sins in accordance with the Scriptures, that he was buried, that he was raised on the third day in accordance with the Scriptures, and that he appeared to Cephas, then to the twelve. Then he appeared to more than five hundred brothers at one time, most of whom are still alive, though some have fallen asleep (that is, have died). Then he appeared to James then to all the apostles. Last of all, as to one untimely born, he appeared also to me" (I Corinthians 15:1–8).

a) The gospel is that Jesus died, was buried, and was raised on the third day.

b) Jesus' death was predicted by Him in the Scriptures.

c) He appeared to Cephas, i.e. Peter.

d) He appeared to the twelve.

e) He appeared to a crowd of five hundred people.

f) He appeared to his half-brother James.

g) He again appeared to all of the Apostles.

h) And Jesus appeared to Paul.

The above is only a partial list of Jesus' appearances as the Gospels mention several other appearances in addition to those mentioned here (I Corinthians 15). Paul, in this text, tells us that Jesus appeared to 527 people. With the other appearances, the number grows to well over 550 people who saw Him alive after His crucifixion, death, embalming and burial. He had been sealed in a tomb for three days and nights before His resurrection. Here is a list of a few additional appearances of Jesus after His resurrection.

A LIST OF OTHER RESURRECTION APPEARANCES

a) Mary Magdalene (Mark 16:-11; John 20:11–18).

b) The other women at the tomb (Matthew 28:8–19; Luke 24:10).

c) Another appearance to Peter in Jerusalem (Luke 24:34).

d) Two travelers on the road to Emmaus (Mark 16:12–13; Luke 24:13–35).

e) Ten disciples behind closed doors (Luke 24:36–43; John 20:19–25).

f) Seven disciples while fishing (John 21:1-14).

g) Eleven disciples on a mountain (Matthew 28:16–20; Mark 16:15–18).

h) Jesus' half-brother James (I Corinthians 15:7).

i) The ascension (Mark 16:19–20; Luke 24:50–53; Acts 1:3–9).

Some have suggested that Jesus might not have really been dead when put in the tomb. But think a moment about that idea—did the Romans not know how to kill a person? Jesus had been severely beaten, probably as many as three times. He had been so savaged He could not even carry His own cross a few hundred yards to Calvary. He had nails driven through His hands and feet. He had his side pierced by a spear and blood and water poured out. Did Roman soldiers not know how to kill a person or when they were dead?

Do you wrap up a person who is not dead in long strips of cloth and then pour 100 pounds of spices on them? Do you seal a live man in a tomb for three days and nights? What about physical needs of elimination and drink? There can be no doubt Jesus was dead.

Trying to deny the events of Jesus' death are a futile effort of someone determined not to believe. If you are struggling with believing, please examine your heart and motives, be honest with yourself. Read again John 3:16–19 and examine your heart.

PENTECOST

Jesus was crucified at the Passover feast. Fifty days later came the feast of Pentecost. The Jews numbered seven full weeks, or 49 days, then on the fiftieth day, Sunday, they celebrated Pentecost (Leviticus 23:16). On Pentecost, Jerusalem and particularly Temple Square were packed with worshipping Jews from around the world.

Let's take up the story in Acts 1:26 and following:

"And they cast lots for them, and the lot fell on Matthias, and he was numbered with the eleven apostles. When the day of Pentecost arrived, they (the Apostles) were all together in one place. And suddenly there came from heaven a sound like a mighty rushing wind, and it filled the entire house where they were sitting .... And they were all filled with the Holy Spirit and began to speak in other tongues as the Spirit gave them utterance. Now there were dwelling in Jerusalem Jews, devout men from every nation under heaven ... Parthians and Medes and Elamites and residents of Mesopotamia, Judea and Cappadocia, Pontus and Asia, Phrygia and Pamphylia, Egypt and parts of Libya belonging to Cyrene, and visitors from Rome, both Jews and proselytes, Cretans and Arabians—we hear them telling in our own tongues the mighty works of god" (Acts 1:26- 2:1–11).

Sixteen nations are mentioned here and when it is known that everyone heard in their own "dialect," the number of different languages could have been as many as 20-30. These Jews, from around the world, would return home with the gospel message. This was the beginning of the gospel being preached internationally.

"But Peter, standing with the eleven, lifted up his voice and addressed them" (Acts 2:14)

Peter gives a brief summary of the prophetic proof that Jesus was the promised Messiah, but they had not understood who He was and had ended up crucifying Him.

> "Let all the House of Israel therefore know for certain that God has made him both Lord and Christ, this Jesus whom you crucified" (Acts 2:36).

> "Now when they heard this they were cut to the heart, and said to Peter and the rest of the apostles, Brothers, 'what shall we do?' And Peter said to them, 'Repent and be baptized every one of you in the name of Jesus Christ for the forgiveness of your sins, and you will receive the gift of the Holy Spirit. For the promise is for you and for your children and for all who are far off, everyone whom the Lord our God calls to himself'... So those who received his word were baptized, and there were added that day about three thousand souls" (Acts 37—39 & 41).

Quite a change had taken place in the minds of these people in just under fifty days. First the crowd was crying "Crucify him, crucify him" at the Passover. Now at Pentecost this same group of people who shouted to have Jesus killed are gathered together in the same place and are convicted of their terrible mistake. What had happened to them to change their minds and hearts? It had to have been climactic.

These same people came to accept Jesus as their Savior and even be baptized. Why? The only explanation that makes sense is that Jesus was in fact resurrected and stayed around Jerusalem many days, and the evidence was so clear that even these Jewish people from around the world, who had come to celebrate their Jewish festivals, were absolutely convinced. When they returned home they were no longer Jewish, but Christians. They had seen positive, irrefutable proof that Jesus was resurrected.

THE FIRST FEW WEEKS IN JERUSALEM

This Christian revival did not stop on the day of Pentecost, but continued on in Jerusalem and around the whole world. Acts records the remarkable growth of the church in Jerusalem.

> "But many of those who had heard the word believed, and the number of the men came to be about five thousand" (Acts 4:4).

Add to this number of men the wives and children and the number easily could have been as much as 20,000 Christians in Jerusalem in just a few weeks. Then it was reported:

> "And more than ever believers were added to the Lord, multitudes of both men and women" (Acts 5:14).

Five thousand male converts was quite impressive, but here the number is expressed as "multitudes of men and women." How many is a multitude? No longer were people being added but the number was now multiplying.

> "Now in these days when the disciples were increasing in number, a complaint by the Hellenists arose ..." "And the word of God continued to increase, and the number of the disciples *multiplied greatly* in Jerusalem, and a *great many of the priests* became obedient to the faith" (Acts 6:1 & 7)

At first people were added, then they were multiplied, and then they were greatly multiplied. Not only the regular Jews were coming to Christ but "a great many of the priests" became Christians. There had to have been an obvious reason for this revival: it was because the resurrection had really happened.

Jerusalem, at the time of the Jewish festivals, swelled to a population of up to one million people. But normally at that time it was a city of about 65,000 people. It is most likely that in a few weeks well over half of those living there were now Christian. Even the Temple service was interrupted due to loss of priests to Christianity. Why? The answer is obvious—Christ was resurrected.

SAMARIA AND BEYOND

"And the crowds with one accord paid attention to what was being said by Philip when they heard him ..." (Acts 8:6) "but when they believed Philip as he preached good news about the kingdom of God and the name of Jesus Christ they were baptized both men and women. Even Simon himself believed, and after being baptized he continued with Philip" (Acts 8:12-13).

This was happening in Samaria as well as in Jerusalem and Judea. Samaria was sort of a second capital in Israel as it had been the capital of the ten tribes when Israel was split by Jeroboam after the death of Solomon. So the message is spreading all over Israel. Both genders are coming to Christ in great numbers and even Simon, who had practiced magic or sorcery, was converted.

CONVERSION OF SAUL AND THE BEGINNING OF FOREIGN MISSIONS

Acts 9 records the conversion of Saul, who later came to be known as Paul. Who was he? He was of the top ruling class or Sanhedrin. He was one of the best educated and outstanding Hebrew scholars of his time. He had persecuted and had been killing the Christians. No myth or fable would have immediately and totally reversed the whole direction of his life. No fact less than the resurrection could explain this drastic change of direction in Paul's life.

GENTILES ARE BEING EVANGELIZED

Acts 10 tells of the first Gentiles being won to Christ with the conversion of Cornelius, a Roman military leader. Peter introduced Christ to the Gentiles and now the gospel is reaching out to all nations. Peter used the keys Jesus had given to him in Matthew 16:18-19 to open the Kingdom doors to the Jews at Pentecost and again he used these keys to open the doors of the Kingdom to the first Gentiles with Cornelius and his household.

Acts 13 tells of the beginning of the missionary movement, with the first of three mission trips led by Paul and his traveling companions. During these mission trips, thousands of people all over Asia Minor and Europe were converted. Paul says that all of Asia, (what we think of as Turkey today), had come to Christ.

Strong churches were planted in Ephesus, Smyrna, Pergamum, Thyatira, Sardis, Philadelphia, and Laodicea, and many smaller churches like the ones at Colossae and Philippi. The large churches were in major population centers in Asia Minor, but even smaller communities have churches.

In Europe churches were being planted in Philippi, Thessaloniki, Athens, and Corinth. How could this have happened if the report of what had happened in Jerusalem had not been widely told by eyewitnesses all over the Empire?

By the time the book of Colossians was written, Paul says:

> "...because of the hope laid up for you in heaven. Of this you have heard before in the word of the truth, the gospel, which has come to you, *as indeed in the **whole world*** it is bearing fruit and increasing—" (Colossians 1:5-6).

> "If indeed you continue in the faith, stable and steadfast, not shifting from the hope of the gospel that you heard **which has been proclaimed in all creation under heaven** and of which I, Paul, became a minister" (Colossians 1:23).

The New Testament only follows the work of a few of the Apostles in Acts and the Epistles. Non-biblical history informs us of the work of the other Apostles. The gospel was preached as far away as India. Thomas was martyred at Madras on the east coast of Southern India.

The gospel was also preached across Africa, Asia, the Far East, Europe, as far as the British Isles, in France, and Spain. Paul is correct in saying that the gospel had been preached in the whole world. Christ's twelve Apostles had fulfilled the directive of Jesus:

> "Go therefore and make disciples of all nations, baptizing them in

the name of the Father and of the Son and of the Holy Spirit, teaching them to observe all that I have commanded you. And behold, I am with you always, to the end of the age" (Matthew 28:19-20).

THE END OF THE FIRST CENTURY

At the end of the first century, the Roman Empire embraced an estimated 220 million citizens and covered the environs of the Mediterranean world and most of Europe and a lot of Africa.

At the end of the first century, there were five centers of Christianity in the Roman world. The first was the church at Jerusalem, second the church at Antioch of Syria, the third was in Alexandria, Egypt, the fourth the Greek Church, and last the Roman church. Four of these ancient churches still remain. Other smaller Christian centers existed in places like Ethiopia, India, and the Far East.

We call the four remaining of these five churches: The Coptic Church of Egypt, the Syrian Orthodox Church of Syria, the Greek Orthodox Church of Greece, and the Roman Catholic Church of Rome, Italy.

The Jerusalem Church was totally wiped out by the Islamic invasion of the Empire that lasted 150 years from A.D. 582-732. The Muslims were finally defeated by Charles Martel at the battle at Tours, France.

But by the end of the work of the Twelve Apostles it is thought that about 25% of the world had been converted to Christianity. Christianity was well represented across India, Africa, the Middle East, Asia Minor, Asia, the Far East, the islands of the sea, and across Europe.

How would a person explain this success of the gospel unless in fact there was absolute positive proof that Jesus was the Messiah and that He was the resurrected Savior of all of humanity?

THE FIRST TO FOURTH CENTURIES

From the mid to latter part of the first century to the first of the fourth century the church suffered massive persecution, with the goal having often been to totally wipe out the Christian church.

One of the worst of these persecutions came under Emperor Nero, and even worse was the one that came by Emperor Diocletian. Diocletian sought to totally remove the Christian community worldwide as well as to wipe out all Bibles, both Old and New Testament.

Millions of Christians were killed in twelve persecutions under ten different emperors. Many very important old biblical texts of both Old and New Testaments were destroyed. Fortunately for us today, many Bible texts survived.

People were slaughtered, beheaded, hung, crucified, crucified upside down, and burned at the stake. It was said during that period that, "the blood of the martyrs became the seeds of the church." The more the church was persecuted the more it grew. The church went underground, meeting in homes, underground in the catacombs, in caves, and out under the stars. The church continued to flourish. Why? The answer is still the same—something wonderful had happened in Jerusalem at the garden tomb of Joseph of Arimathea—Jesus the Messiah was resurrected from the dead. The proof was clear then and is even clearer for us today.

EMPEROR CONSTANTINE IN THE FOURTH CENTURY

About A.D. 312, Constantine won control of the Roman Empire by defeating Maxentius Licenius, who was drowned in the Tiber River. Constantine's mother, Helena, was a nominal Christian. Although probably not totally dedicated, she was a believer. During one of the final great battles fought by Constantine, he claimed to have seen a large cross in the clouds and went on to decisively win the battle and to become Emperor of the Roman Empire. From this event he also came to believe that Jesus was the Messiah.

Constantine wished for his whole army to become Christians and marched them down through the sea, claiming to have baptized them all. He had zeal for promoting the Christian faith and gave the edict of toleration in A.D. 312, permitting people to openly be Christians and then the Edict of Milan in 330 when he made Christianity the official religion of the whole Empire.

He gave gifts to those who claimed to have become Christians, probably new clothes and money. A huge influx of people swarmed into the church. This was both a blessing and a curse. The result was that people came into the church without really being born again. They brought with them a lot from their idolatry; incense burning, idols, worship of the dead or animism, praying to dead people, worship of Mary, Jesus' mother, and a score of other evils. This ended up beginning the corruption of the church doctrinally/spiritually and ushered in the Dark Ages. Much more could be said about this but is not primarily relevant to our present discussion.

Constantine moved the capital of the Empire from Rome to Constantinople. He built a glorious church there called "Saint Sophia" or "St. Wisdom." During a thunder storm it was struck by lightning and burned down. It was rebuilt with the same result the second time. Both of these buildings were made of wood. Finally, Emperor Justinian, in A.D. 537, built the third and final St. Sophia that remains to this day.

For 1,000 years St. Sophia was the largest building on earth. It has gained the attention of people world-wide from its inception, and even still today. It is said to hold up to 65,000 people for church and yes, it had, and still has, an immersion baptistery.

By the fourth century, Christianity had become the religion of the whole Roman Empire. Some estimates of the number of believers are as high as 75% of the Empire, or 187,500,000 Christians just in the Roman world. This does not take into account the millions in other far off nations.

The question is, why such a massive impact on the world? By the time of the Apostle John's death, about 25% of the known world were Christians and then by the time of Emperor Constantine, 75% of the Empire were Christians.

Why did all this happen? It was because of the ministry of Jesus and the crowning event of His death, burial, and resurrection. It can be traced back to an empty tomb at Jerusalem. Christians do not go to a dead man's tomb to ask questions about life after death. They listen to and get their directions from the resurrected Messiah.

WHAT WE NOW KNOW FOR SURE

There are three truths we can know for sure today:

BIBLICAL ACCURACY

Truth one: The Bible is accurate and true

First, we know that the Holy Bible has been faithfully handed down to us today. Those who were responsible for copying it knew these were the actual words of God and they as custodians were entrusted with its safe transmission. This was the primary function of the scribes.

We today have thousands of biblical manuscripts and with so many, yes, there are variant readings. I have spent a lifetime studying biblical manuscripts and have found no significant biblical teaching in the Old or New Testament that can be brought into question because of manuscript variant reading.

The Isaiah Dead Sea Scroll dates to 268 B.C. and between it and the Leningrad Hebrew text of A.D. 1017, the variant readings are so minute as to be of interest only to biblical scholars. We have no doubt about what was said by Isaiah. It had been faithfully copied for 1,300 years.

THE ANVIL OF GOD'S WORD

Last even I paused beside the blacksmith's door,
    And heard the anvil ring the vesper chime;
Then looking in, I saw upon the floor,
    Old hammers worn with beating years of time.

"How many anvils have you had," said I,
   "To wear and batter all these hammers so?"
"Just one," said he, and then with twinkling eye,
   "The anvil wears the hammers out, you know."

"And so," I thought, "The Anvil of God's Word,
   For ages skeptic blows have beat upon,
Yet, though the sound of falling blows was heard,
   The anvil is unharmed, the hammers gone.
      Robert B. Pattison

The end of the matter is that your Bible is marvelously accurate and reliable. For a full treatment of this subject please see *The Bible: the True and Reliable Word of God*, by Dr. Charles A. Crane, Endurance Press, Star, Idaho.

353 JESUS PROPHECIES FOUND IN THE OLD TESTAMENT

Truth two: Prophecy proves who Jesus was and is

A list has been given of 353 prophecies of Jesus' coming that are found in the Old Testament which are quoted in the New Testament. In reality there are about 500 actual prophecies and in addition to these we have shown there are about 7,000 references to Jesus in the 39 books of the Old Testament.

Today we know for sure that these are prophecies. Jesus' whole history can be told from quoting the old prophets. They told of His conception, birth, boyhood, life, teaching, death, and His resurrection.

Prophecy is positive proof that Jesus was who He said He was. It is irrefutable, undeniable, and certain proof that He is the Messiah. To deny these obvious proofs of who He was and what He did shows those that still reject Him either do not know the facts, but if they know and still reject Him it is because their hearts are evil (John 3:19).

THE RESURRECTION

Truth three: the resurrection gives irrefutable proof that Jesus is the Messiah

Jesus' death was probably the most awful low point in human history—three times beaten with a cat of nine tails, abused, malnourished, cast into a pit all night with lacerated back, and finally, the most awful possible thing, He was cut off from the Father, the first human to be cast down into Hades. The Holy Trinity was temporarily broken and the sins of the whole world, past, present, and future, were cast upon Him. Certainly it was the darkest day of all human history. In all history no other person has suffered like Jesus. Five trials, betrayal of His friends and Apostles, whipped two or three times, thrown into the pit below the High Priest's house, and finally in His death He had almost nothing left. He was stretched between earth and sky, naked, crucified, nails driven through His hands and feet. A spear pierced His side and then in anguish He died. But out of His suffering came our redemption.

If Jesus was only a man He could have only paid for one man's sins, but no, He was God, the owner and creator of the universe. He owned everything and was worth more than everything. He was of more value than all humanity. He paid the price in full for all who will accept Him. In the end He was stripped of everything but His crown of thorns and His cross.

THE CROSS WAS HIS OWN

They borrowed a bed to lay His head,
    When Christ the Lord came down,
They borrowed the ass in the mountain pass:
    For Him to ride to town:

But the crown that He wore,
    And the cross He bore were His own—
The cross was His own.

He borrowed the bread when the crowd He fed,
    On the grassy mountain side,
He borrowed the dish of broken fish,
    With which He satisfied;
But the crown that He wore,
    And the cross that He bore, were His own—
The cross was His own.

He borrowed the ship in which to sit,
    To teach the multitude.
He borrowed a nest in which to rest,
    He had never a home so rude:
But the crown that He wore,
    And the cross that He bore, were His own—
The cross was His own.

He borrowed a room on His way to the tomb,
    The passion lamb to eat,
They borrowed a cave for Him a grave,
    They borrowed a winding sheet:
But the crown that He wore,
    And the cross that He bore, were His own—
The cross was His own.
        Author unknown

His death seemed like the final page in His life of sorrow and deprivation. It seemed that Satan had won the match that had its beginning in the Garden of Eden, but not so, for three days later death was vanquished as Jesus arose triumphant from the grave as the first fruit of the resurrection and proof that we humans can have eternal life. Up from the grave He arose! His feet were pierced but Satan's head was crushed.

The final truth that proves Jesus is the Messiah is His resurrection. A short summary of the evidence for the resurrection has been given—Pentecost, 550 eye witnesses, 3,000 Jews baptized just 50 days after his crucifixion.

Then fifty days after His resurrection, at Pentecost, began the remarkable spread of Christianity over the whole earth before the last of the twelve Apostles had died. This could not have happened without there being an empty tomb in Jerusalem with the words written outside, "He is not here, for He has risen, come see the place where He lay."

Today Christianity still marches forward on all continents and in all nations. Yes, it is still persecuted and many reject it. But the truth marches on, lives are changed and people live and die victoriously around the world. In our often dark world the gospel light still burns brightly. For all who believe have eternal life.

> "For God so loved the world that He gave His only begotten Son that whosoever believeth in Him shall have everlasting life" (John 3:16).

A CALL TO FAITH

There is no one so bad or so good that they do not need to know the living Messiah, Jesus. Jesus still invites, "Come unto me all you who labor and are heavy laden and I will give you rest" (Matthew 11:28).

The whole purpose of this book is to show how firm a foundation the gospel message has so that no one need reject the gospel and end up in Hell.

> "The Lord is not slow to fulfill his promise as some count slowness, but is patient toward you, not wishing that any should perish, but that all should reach repentance" (II Peter 3:9)

God wants no one to go to Hell. It is Peter who reminds us of God's love, he who had cursed and sworn, he who had denied the Lord three times in one night, he understood that God is most merciful to sinners like him and us.

What more proof could God have given us than the Old Testament scriptures so carefully preserved, and today have been proven to be accurate? These 39 Old Testament books are filled with predictions of His coming and thousands of encounters with Jesus the Messiah.

The proofs that Jesus is the Messiah are conclusive. Why would anyone still reject Him with this overpowering evidence? Jesus Himself explains why:

> "For God so loved the world, that he gave his only Son, that whoever believes in him should not perish but have eternal life. For God did not send his Son into the world to condemn the world, but in order that the world might be saved through him. Whoever believes in him is not condemned, but whoever does not believe is condemned already, because he has not believed in the name of the only Son of God. And this is the judgment: the light has come into the world, and people loved the darkness rather than the light because their works were evil. For everyone who does wicked things hates the light and does not come to the light, lest his works should be exposed" (John 3:16–20).

The diagnosis of the creator and great physician, Jesus, may appear harsh, but nevertheless it is true. I puzzled for many years as to why some people seem hardened against the good news of the gospel. Why do they seem so blind, so resistant, so unbelieving? Jesus explains why, because "their works, their hearts are evil." They have become victims of Satan and believe his lies. This lets them do anything their evil hearts want to do, not realizing they are headed to Hell.

This kind of person would make Hell out of Heaven if allowed to go there. Jesus, in His last act of love for them, lets them have what they want and have given their lives to. They have heard the gospel message, gospel music, and the pleas of their fathers, mothers, and grandmothers. They have driven past churches for years. They may have casually participated in Easter and

Christmas. But so often these people have rejected sermons, soul winners, and countless prayers on their behalf, and it is almost as if they have stood and looked at Jesus hanging on the cross and replied with their whole lives, "NO! I will not believe!" They burn out their lives to the end of the candle and fall into a Christless grave, still unrepentant and rejecting the pleading of the Lord Jesus, "Come unto me all you who labor and are heavy laden and I will give you rest."

While in high school, the Superintendent made fun of me, claiming that he was better than the preachers in town, better that any Christian he knew, and he did not need a savior. On the surface this puzzled me as it did appear that he was moral, kind, clean, did not swear, and from all appearances was a really nice person.

It was a shock, a few years later, when another graduate from my class became a stripper and did naked dancing. She was the neighbor girl when I was in grade school. She told me, "Oh, Mr. Maloney, (not his real name) is one of my best customers. He comes and watches me strip down and puts money in my bra and panties." He, a married man—on the surface he looked pretty good but inside his heart was given to lust and lasciviousness. Yes, Jesus knows what He is talking about. People who reject Him have a heart problem. Their hearts are evil.

Over and over again this example of what is in the hearts of the Christ rejecters has repeatedly been confirmed. Yes, Jesus knows everyone's hearts and the creator gives the diagnosis, "Their works are evil ... they hate the light, lest their works be exposed" (John 3:19).

Fortunately, that is not the end of the matter. Even for the most hardened sinner, repentance and accepting Christ can wipe the slate of sins clean. Our sinful hearts can be washed as white as snow. History is full of the accounts of some horribly wicked people who have turned from wasted lives to accept Jesus and do marvelous works of righteousness.

Jerry McCauley

Some people of awful pasts have become powerful Christians. One of these was Jerry McCauley of New York State, who was convicted of seven felonies and was a seven termer in the New York State Prison, but while serving his seventh term was given a Bible that he studied, and he submitted to Jesus Christ. When he was released he began to preach the gospel and led 250,000 New Yorkers to Christ. One writer said, "Jerry McCauley has more power with God and man than all the preachers of metropolitan New York City combined."

The Apostle Paul turned from killing Christians to become one of the greatest preachers and missionaries the world has known. Yes, Jesus can use everyone and He takes our wasted lives and makes something beautiful out of them.

Daniel Webster

The well-known congressman, Daniel Webster, was out to lunch with some of his Congressional colleagues and his friends observed that he was deep in thought and not entering into the conversation. Finally one of his friends said, "Daniel, what is occupying your mind, why are you so deep in thought?"

Daniel the eminent statesman replied, "I am thinking of the greatest theological truth I have ever heard and learned."

His friend asked, "And what would that be?"

Daniel replied, "Jesus loves me, this I know, for the Bible tells me so."

Marcia

At this point in writing this book I was called away from the desk to go to the hospital. A dear friend, Gary, called and said to me, "Could you come to the hospital, Marcia has been given less than two hours to live."

Of course I rushed to the hospital and outside the room the physician told me she was fading fast and nothing could be done to alter her impending death.

Who was Marcia? She was one of the most precious, beautiful, saints of

God, in this very large church. She was not only beautiful but her life was a shining light for Jesus. She was full of good works, helping the weak, old, suffering, baking cookies for Mission Mojo, a Chinese mission project, working as hostess and receptionist in the church offices and always so bright and alive.

When I came into the room her face shone with joy and she said, "Oh, how great to have you come to be with me and Gary." We talked about heaven and how she would soon pass from death and pain into a glorious eternity. After about ninety minutes, with a smile on her face, she closed her eyes as if to go to sleep, took a few deep breaths and passed into her forever life. She died as happy as if tomorrow would be the happiest day of her whole life, and it was.

Mike

While on vacation in Arizona, late one night two years ago, my cell phone rang and it was a dear friend who asked me to call her brother, which I did. I was about to hear a terrible tale of woe.

He told me his name was Mike and that he had come to the end of his life and was set out to commit suicide. He explained how he had lived a selfish life of immorality, drunkenness, drugs, and sin. I asked about his problems and he said he was headed out to the freeway to jump off an overpass in front of a truck.

I asked him to tell me more about his situation and he told me this tragic tale of woe. He said he was 54 and that his whole life was collapsing around him. He was out drinking trying to find some peace and after spending his last dollar went out to get in his car and drive home. But his car was gone; it had been repossessed for lack of payment.

The only person he knew to call was his sister in another state, as his friends had all left him as his life was falling apart. I visited with him for about an hour and then we prayed as he stood beside the freeway. I prayed that someone would stop and give him a ride home and while we were praying a car pulled up and asked how he could help. This Good Samaritan gave him a ride home and I heard nothing more from Mike for three or four months.

His sister called one day to tell me that Mike had moved to her home as he was ill with incurable cancer. She asked if I would come and pray with him, which I did. He insisted he did not believe in any God and besides, he had committed so many sins he was sure God would not help him, nor did he want help from God.

A lady friend of his sister's came to visit Mike. She had been in a class I had taught on how to teach an unsaved person the Roman Road to Salvation, which is a summary of the Bible book of Romans. She insisted that Mike listen to her. Half way through the study Mike said he was too tired to go on. She said, "Mike, you are dying, just be quiet and listen." She finished the half hour lesson. She came back a few days later asking him to re-read the scriptures she had covered.

At that visit Mike ended up confessing his faith in Jesus Christ, saying he had never understood how to be saved and that he was surprised that sinners like him were welcome to come to Christ. I was called and reviewed what Mike had been taught from the book of Romans, and talked to him about being baptized. Again Mike confessed his faith in Jesus.

Although Mike was bedfast, it was arranged for Mike to be baptized the next morning at ten o'clock. When Mike came to the church, it took about twenty minutes to get him from the car to the baptistery. When he was there we prayed and his sister and I helped him into the baptistery. This took another ten minutes. He almost had to be carried down the steps into the warm water.

Together she and I baptized him, and as he came up out of the water he was praising God and thanking him for salvation. He climbed up the stairs all by himself, and walked unaided to the dressing room, changed his clothes without help, and walked two-thirds of the way back to the car when he finally needed the wheel chair to make it the rest of the way to the car. All the way to the car Mike had a big smile and was thanking and praising God.

During the next two weeks Mike was a new person, happy, trusting God and not afraid to die, which he did two weeks later. He had truly been born again.

His funeral was a time of rejoicing, as all of those who knew him realized that he had passed from death into life just before his physical death. He had come into the vineyard of the Lord in the last ten minutes of the day and had been welcomed into the joys of eternal life through Jesus Christ his Lord. There is no sinner who is so bad as to not be welcomed to salvation in Jesus Christ.

Marcia and Mike's faith were not founded on folklore and fables, but on the solid rock of Jesus Christ and the absolute historical truths upon which every Christian's faith rests. My parting words to Mike and Marcia were, "We will be seeing you soon!"

For over sixty years now, ministry has placed me at the bedside of dying Christian people. Mike and Marcia's story has been played out over and over again. All of us in reality are terminal; we just do not know the day or hour. It is so important that we accept Jesus' offer of eternal life. The facts are in, He is the Messiah, He is Jesus Christ, the savior of all humanity, for all that will accept Him.

How glorious are the deaths of the righteous and how exceedingly awful the death of the unbeliever. God has no joy in the death of the wicked. But to as many as accept Him to them He gives eternal life.

WHAT A FRIEND WE HAVE IN JESUS

What a friend we have in Jesus,
All our sins and griefs to bear!
What a privilege to carry
Everything to God in prayer!
Oh, what peace we often forfeit,
Oh, what needless pain we bear,
All because we do not carry
Everything to God in prayer!

Have we trials and temptations?
Is there trouble anywhere?
We should never be discouraged—
Take it to the Lord in prayer.
Can we find a friend so faithful,
Who will all our sorrows share?
Jesus knows our every weakness;
Take it to the Lord in prayer.

Are we weak and heavy-laden,
Cumbered with a load of care?
Precious Savior, still our refuge—
Take it to the Lord in prayer.
Do thy friends despise, forsake thee?
Take it to the Lord in prayer!
In His arms He'll take and shield thee,
Thou wilt find a solace there.

Blessed Savior, Thou hast promised
Thou wilt all our burdens bear;
May we ever, Lord, be bringing
All to Thee in earnest prayer.
Soon in glory bright, unclouded,
There will be no need for prayer—
Rapture, praise, and endless worship,
Will be our sweet portions there.
Joseph M. Scriven

The proof that Jesus is the Christ, the Messiah and Savior of all mankind is absolute, irrefutable, beyond doubt. Why would any person refuse His offer of salvation? "For God so loved the world that he gave his only begotten son, that whosoever believeth in him should not perish but have everlasting life" (John 3:16).

THE DEADLINE

There is a time, I know not when,
    A place, I know not where,
Which marks the destiny of men
    To Heaven or despair.

There is a line by us not seen,
    Which crosses every path;
The hidden boundary between
    God's patience and His wrath.

To cross that limit is to die,
    To die, as if by stealth.
It may not pale the beaming eye,
    Nor quench the glowing health.

The conscience may be still at ease,
    The spirit light and gay.
That which is pleasing still may please,
    And care be thrust away.

But on that forehead God hath set
    Indelibly a mark,
By man unseen, for man as yet
    Is blind and in the dark.

And still the doomed man's path below
    May bloom like Eden bloomed.
He did not, does not, will not know,
    Nor feel that he is doomed.

He feels, he sees that all is well,
    His every fear is calmed.
He lives, he dies, he wakes in Hell,
    Not only doomed, but damned.

Oh, where is that mysterious bourn,
    By which each path is crossed,
Beyond which God Himself hath sworn
    That he who goes is lost?

How long may man go on in sin,
    How long will God forbear?
Where does hope end, and where begin
    The confines of despair?

One answer from the sky is sent,
    Ye who from God depart,
While it is called today, repent
    And harden not your heart.

Please accept His offer of salvation while you may! Jesus is the Messiah and this truth is founded on many irrefutable proofs!

THERE ALWAYS WILL BE GOD

They cannot shell His temple,
    Nor dynamite His throne;
They cannot bomb His city,
    Nor rob Him of His own

They cannot take Him captive,
    Nor strike Him deaf and blind,
Nor starve Him to surrender,
    Nor make Him change His mind.

They cannot cause Him panic;
    Nor cut off His supplies;
They cannot take His kingdom,
    Nor hurt Him with their lives.

Though all the world be shattered,
    His truth remains the same,
His righteous laws will still potent,
    And "Father" still His name.

Though we face war and struggle
    And feel their goad and rod,
We know above confusion
    There always will be God.
    Dr. Albert Murry

We live and rest in peace knowing Jesus is the Messiah and that He is our Lord and Savior. As Christians we have already passed from death into life (John 3:16 and 10:10).

APPENDIX

Old Testament Messianic Prophecies Fulfilled Concerning Jesus Christ

ALL of these prophesies were made hundreds, some thousands, of years before Jesus Christ was born. Looking in the face of how He literally fulfilled them all (plus hundreds more), it is an impossibility that He is not Messiah, Savior of the world. The ONLY person ... past, present or future ... who could fulfill all these prophecies is Jesus Christ. See His genealogy starting from faithful Abraham.

Fulfilled Prophecy	Tenakh/Hebrew Scripture	New Testament
His pre-existence	Micah 5:2	John 1:1, 14
Born of the seed of a woman	Genesis 3:15	Matthew 1:18
Of the seed of Abraham	Genesis 12:3	Matthew 1:1–16
All nations blessed by Abraham's seed	Genesis 12:3	Matthew 8:5, 10
God would provide Himself a Lamb as an offering	Genesis 22:8	John 1:29
From the tribe of Judah	Genesis 49:10	Matthew 1:1–3
Heir to the throne of David	Isaiah 9:6–7	Matthew 1:1
Called "The mighty God, The everlasting Father"	Isaiah 9:6	Matthew 1:23
Born in Bethlehem	Micah 5:2	Matthew 2:1
Born of a virgin	Isaiah 7:14	Matthew 1:18
His name called Immanuel, "God with us"	Isaiah 7:14	Matthew 1:23
Declared to be the Son of God	Psalm 2:7	Matthew 3:17
His messenger before Him in spirit of Elijah	Malach 4:5–6	Luke 1:17
Preceded by a messenger to prepare His way	Malachi 3:1	Matthew 11:7–11

Messenger crying "Prepare ye the way of the Lord"	Isaiah 40:3	Matthew 11:7–11
Would be a Prophet of the children of Israel	Dueteronomy 18:15	Matthew 2:15
Called out of Egypt	Hosea 11:1	Matthew 2:15
Slaughter of the children	Jeremiah 31:1	Matthew 2:18
Would be a Nazarene	Judges 13:5; Amos 2:11; Lamentations 4:7	Matthew 2:23
Brought light to Zabulon and Nephthalm, Galilee of the Gentiles	Isaiah 9:1–2	Matthew 4:15
Presented with gifts	Psalm 72:10	Matthew 2:1, 11
Rejected by His own	Isaiah 53:3	Matthew 21:42: Mark 8:31, 12:10; Luke 9:22, 17:25
He is the stone which the builders rejected which became the headstone	Psalm 118:22–23, Isaiah 28:16	Matthew 21:42, 1 Peter 2:7
A stone of stumbling to Israel	Isaiah 8:14–15	1 Peter 2:8
He entered Jerusalem as a king riding on an ass	Zechariah 9:9	Matthew 21:5
Betrayed by a friend	Psalm 41:9	John 13:21
Sold for 30 pieces of silver	Zechariah 11:12	Matthew 26:15; Luke 22:5
The 30 pieces of silver given for the potter's field	Zechariah 11:12	Matthew 27:9–10
The 30 pieces of silver thrown in the temple	Zechariah 11:13	Matthew 27:5
Forsaken by His disciples	Zechariah 13:7	Matthew 26:56
Accused by false witnesses	Psalm 35:11	Matthew 26:60
Silent to accusations	Isaiah 53:7	Matthew 27:14
Heal blind/deaf/lame/dumb	Isaiah 35:5–6; Isaiah 29:18	Matthew 11:5
Preached to the poor/ broken hearted/ captives	Isaiah 61:1	Matthew 11:5
Came to bring a sword, not peace	Micah 7:6	Matthew 10:34–35
He bore our sickness	Isaiah 53:4	Matthew 8:16–17
Spat upon, smitten and scourged	Isaiah 50:6, 53:5	Matthew 27:26, 30
Smitten on the cheek	Micah 5:1	Matthew 27:30

Hated without a cause	Psalm 35:18	Matthew 27:23
The sacrificial lamb	Isaiah 53:5	John 1:29
Given for a covenant		
Would not strive or cry	Isaiah 42:2-3	Mark 7:36
People would hear not and see not	Isaiah 6:9-10	Matthew 13:14-15
People trust in traditions of men	Isaiah 29:13	Matthew 15:9
People give God lip service	Isaiah 29:13	Matthew 15:8
God delights in Him	Isaiah 42:1	Matthew 3:17, 17:5
Wounded for our sins	Isaiah 53:5	John 6:51
He bore the sins of many	Isaiah 53:10-12	Mark 10:45
Messiah not killed for Himself	Daniel 9:26	Matthew 20:28
Gentiles flock to Him	Isaiah 55:5, 60:3, 65:1; Malachi 1:11; 2 Samuel 22:44-45; Psalm 2:7-8	Matthew 8:10
Crucified with criminals	Isaiah 53:12	Matthew 27:35
His body was pierced	Zechariah 12:10; Ps. 22:16	John 20:25, 27
Thirsty during execution	Psalm 22:15	John 19:28
Given vinegar and gall for thirst	Psalm 69:23	Matthew 27:34
Soldiers gambled for his garment	Psalm 22:18	Matthew 27:35
People mocked, "He trusted in God, let Him deliver him!"	Psalm 22:7-8	Matthew 27:43
People sat there looking at Him	Psalm 22:17	Matthew 27:36
Cried, "My God, my God why hast thou forsaken me?"	Psalm 22:1	Matthew 27:46
Darkness over the land	Amos 8:9	Matthew 27:45
No bones broken	Psalm 34:20; Numbers 9:12	John 19:33-36
Side pierced	Zechariah 12:10	John 19:34
Buried with the rich	Isaiah 53:9	Matthew 27:57, 60
Resurrected from the dead	Psalm 16:10-11, 49:15	Mark 16:6
Priest after the order of Melchizedek	Psalm 110:4	Hebrews 5:5-6, 6:20, 7:15-17
Ascended to right hand of God	Psalm 68:18	Luke 24:51
LORD said unto Him, "Sit thou at my right hand, until I make thine enemies thy footstool	Psalm 110:1	Matthew 22:44; Mark 12:36, 16:19; Luke 20:42-43; Acts 2:34-35 Hebrews 1:13
His coming glory	Malachi 3:2-3	Luke 3:17

324 Messianic Prophecies

Gen. 3:15 ..... He will bruise Satan's head ..... Heb. 2:14, 1 Jn. 3:18
Gen. 5:24 .... The bodily ascension to heaven illustrated .... Mk. 6:19
Gen. 9:26, 27 ... The God of Shem will be the Son of Shem ... Lu. 3:36
Gen. 12:3 ... As Abraham's seed, will bless all nations ... Acts. 3:25, 26
Gen. 12:7 ... **The Promise made to Abraham's Seed** ... Gal. 3:16
Gen. 14:18 ... A priest after Melchizedek ... Heb. 6:20
Gen. 14:18 ... A King also ... Heb. 7:2
Gen. 14:18 ... The Last Supper foreshadowed ... Mt. 26:26–29
Gen. 17:19 ... **The Seed of Isaac** ... Rom. 9:7
Gen. 22:8 ... The Lamb of God promised ... Jn. 1:29
Gen. 22:18 ... As Isaac's seed, will bless all nations ... Gal. 3:16
Gen. 26:2–5 ... The Seed of Isaac promised as the Redeemer ... Heb.11:18
Gen. 49:10 ... The time of His coming ... Lu. 2:1–7; Gal. 4:4
Gen. 49:10 ... **The Seed of Judah** ... Lu. 3:33
Gen. 49:10 ... Called Shiloh or One Sent ... Jn. 17:3
Gen. 49:10 ... To come before Judah lost identity ... Jn. 11:47–52
Gen. 49:10 ... To Him shall the obedience of the people be ... Jn. 10:16
Ex. 3:13, 14 ... The Great "I Am" ... Jn. 4:26
Ex. 12:5 ... A Lamb without blemish ... 1 Pet. 1:19
Ex. 12:13 ... The blood of the Lamb saves from wrath ... Rom. 5:8
Ex. 12:21–27 ... Christ is our Passover ... 1 Cor. 5;7
Ex. 12:46 ... **Not a bone of the Lamb to be broken** ... Jn. 19:31–36
Ex. 15:2 ... His exaltation predicted as Yeshua ... Acts 7:55, 56
Ex. 15:11 ... His Character—Holiness ... Luke 1:35; Acts 4:27
Ex. 17:6 ... The Spiritual Rock of Israel ... 1 Cor. 10;4
Ex. 33:19 ... His Character—Merciful ... Lu. 1:72
Lev. 14:11 .. The leper cleansed—Sign to priesthood .. Lu. 5: 12–14; Acts 6:7
Lev. 16:15–17 ... Prefigures Christ's once-for-all death ... Heb. 9:7–14
Lev. 16:27 ... Suffering outside the Camp ... Mt. 27:33; Heb. 13:11, 12
Lev. 17:11 ... The Blood—the life of the flesh ... Mt. 26:28; Mk. 10:45
Lev. 17:11 ... **It is the blood that makes atonement** ... 1 Jn. 3: 14–18
Lev. 23:36–37 ... The Drink-offering: "If any man thirst." .. Jn. 19:31–36
Num. 9:12 ... **Not a bone of Him broken** ... John 19:31–36
Num. 21:9 ... The serpent on a pole—Christ lifted up ... Jn. 3:14–18
Num. 24:17 ... Time: "I shall see him, but not now." ... Gal. 4:4
Deut. 18:15 ... "This is of a truth that prophet." ... Jn. 6:14
Deut. 18:15–16 ... "Had ye believed Moses, ye would believe me." ... Jn. 5:45–47

Deut. 18:18 ... Sent by the Father to speak His word ... Jn. 8:28, 29
Deut. 18:19 ... Whoever will not hear must bear his sin ... Jn. 12:15,
Deut. 21:23 ... Cursed is he that hangs on a tree ... Gal. 3:10–13
Ruth 4:4–9 ... Christ, our kinsman, has redeemed us ... Eph. 1 :3–7
1 Sam. 2:10 ... Shall be an anointed King to the Lord ... Mt. 28:18; Jn. 12:15
2 Sam. 7:12 ... **David's Seed** ... Mt. 1:1
2 Sam. 7:14a ... The Son of God ... Lu. 1:32
2 Sam. 7:16 ... David's house established forever ... Lu. 3:31; Rev. 22:16
2 Ki. 2:11 ... The bodily ascension to heaven illustrated ... Lu. 24:51
1 Chr. 17:11 ... David's Seed ... Mt. 1:1; 9:27
1 Chr. 17:12, 13a ... To reign on David's throne forever ... Lu. 1: 32, 33
1 Chr. 17:13a ... "I will be His Father, He ... my Son." ... Heb. 1:5
Job 19:23–27 ... The Resurrection predicted ... Jn. 5:24-29
Psa. 2:1–3 ... The enmity of kings foreordained ... Acts 4:25–28
Psa. 2:2 ... To own the title, Anointed (Christ) ... Acts 2:36
Psa. 2:6 ... His Character—Holiness ... Jn. 8:46; Rev. 3:7
Psa. 2:6 ... To own the title King ... Mt. 2:2
Psa. 2:7 ... **Declared the Beloved Son** ... Mt. 3;17
Psa. 2:7, 8 ... The Crucifixion and Resurrection intimated ... Acts 13:29–33
Psa. 2:12 ... Life comes through faith in Him ... Jn. 20:31
Psa. 8:2 ... The mouths of babes perfect His praise ... Mt. 21 :16
Psa. 8:5, 6 ... His humiliation and exaltation ... Lu. 24:50–53; 1 Cor. 15:27
Psa. 16:10 ... **Was not to see corruption** ... Acts 2:31
Psa. 16:9–11 ... **Was to arise from the dead** ... Jn. 20:9
Psa. 17:15 ... The resurrection predicted ... Lu. 24:6
Psa. 22:1 ... **Forsaken because of sins of others** ... 2 Cor. 5:21
Psa. 22:1 ... **Words spoken from Calvary, "My God"** ... Mk. 15:34
Psa. 22:2 ... **Darkness upon Calvary** ... Mt. 27:45
Psa. 22:7 ... **They shoot out the lip and shake the head** ... Mt. 27:39
Psa. 22:8 .. **"He trusted in God, let Him deliver Him"** ... Mt. 27:43
Psa. 22:9 ... **Born the Saviour** ... Lu. 2:7
Psa. 22:14 ... **Died of a broken (ruptured)heart** ... Jn. 19:34
Psa. 22:14, 15 ... **Suffered agony on Calvary** ... Mk. 15:34–37
Psa. 22:15 ... **He thirsted** ... Jn. 19:28
Psa. 22:16 ... **They pierced His hands and His feet** .... Jn. 19: 34,37;20:27
Psa. 22:17, 18 ... **Stripped Him before the stares of men** ... Lu. 23:34,35
Psa. 22:18 ..... **They parted His garments** ..... Jn. 19:23,24
Psa. 22:20, 21 ... **He committed Himself to God** ... Lu.23:46
Psa. 22:20, 21 ... **Satanic power bruising the Redeemer's heel** ...Heb. 2:14

Psa. 22:22 ..... **His Resurrection declared** ..... Jn. 20: 17
Psa. 22:27 ... **He shall be the governor of the nations** ... Col 1: 16
Psa. 22:31 ... **"It is finished"** ... Jn. 19:30
Psa. 23:1 .... "I am the Good Shepherd" .... Jn. 10:11
Psa. 24:3 ... His exaltation predicted ... Acts 1 :11; Phil. 2:9
Psa. 30:3 ... His resurrection predicted ... Acts 2:32
Psa. 31 :5 ... **"Into thy hands I commit my spirit"** ... Lu. 23:46
Psa. 31 :11 ... His acquaintances fled from Him ... Mk. 14:50
Psa. 31: 13 ... They took counsel to put Him to death ... Jn. 11:53
Psa. 31 :14, 15 ... " He trusted in God, let Him deliver him" ... Mt. 27:43
Psa. 34:20 ... Not a bone of Him broken ... Jn 19:31–36
Psa. 35:11 ... False witnesses rose up against Him .... Mt. 26:59
Psa. 35: 19 ... He was hated without a cause ... Jn. 15:25
Psa. 38: 11 ... His friends stood afar off ... Lu. 23:49
Psa. 40:2–5 ... The joy of His resurrection predicted ... Jn. 20:20
Psa. 40:6-8 ... His delight—the will of the Father ... Jn. 4:34
Psa. 40:9 .... He was to preach the Righteousness in Israel. ... Mt. 4:17
Psa. 40:14 ... Confronted by adversaries in the Garden ... Jn. 18:4–6
Psa. 41:9 ... Betrayed by a familiar friend ... Jn. 13:18
Psa. 45:2 ... Words of Grace come from His lips ... Lu. 4:22
Psa. 45:6 ... To own the title, God or Elohim ... Heb. 1 :8
Psa. 45:7 ... A special anointing by the Holy Spirit ... Mt.3:16; Heb.1:9
Psa. 45:7, 8 ... Called the Christ (Messiah or Anointed) ... Lu. 2:11
Psa. 55:12–14 ... Betrayed by a friend, not an enemy ... Jn. 13:18
Psa. 55:15 ... Unrepentant death of the Betrayer ... Mt. 27: 3–5; Acts 1: 16–19
Psa. 68:18 ... To give gifts to men ... Eph. 4:7-16
Psa. 68:18 ... Ascended into Heaven ... Lu. 24:51
Psa. 69:4 ... Hated without a cause ... Jn. 15:25
Psa. 69:8 ... A stranger to own brethren ... Lu. 8;20,21
Psa. 69:9 ... Zealous for the Lord's House ... Jn. 2:17
Psa. 69:14–20 ... Messiah's anguish of soul before crucifixion ... Mt. 26:36–45
Psa. 69:20 ... "My soul is exceeding sorrowful." ... Mt. 26:38
Psa. 69:21 ... Given vinegar in thirst ... Mt. 27:34
Psa. 69:26 ... The Saviour given and smitten by God ... Jn. 17:4; 18: 11
Psa. 72:10, 11 ... Great persons were to visit Him ... Mt. 2:1–11
Psa. 72:16 ... The corn of wheat to fall into the Ground ... Jn. 12:24
Psa. 72:17 ... His name, Yinon, will produce offspring ... Jn. 1:12,13
Psa. 72:17 ... All nations shall be blessed by Him ... Acts 2:11, 12,41
Psa. 78:1.2 ... He would teach in parables ... Mt. 13:34–35
Psa. 78:2b ... To speak the Wisdom of God with authority ... Mt. 7:29

Psa. 88:8 ... They stood afar off and watched ... Lu. 23:49
Psa. 89:27 ... Emmanuel to be higher than earthly kings ... Lu. 1:32,33
Psa. 89:35–37 ... David's Seed, throne, kingdom endure forever. .. Lu.1:32,33
Psa. 89:36–37 ... His character—Faithfulness ... Rev. 1:5
Psa. 90:2 ... He is from everlasting (Micah 5:2) ... Jn. 1:1
Psa. 91: 11, 12 ... Identified as Messianic; used to tempt Christ ... Lu. 4;10,11
Psa. 97:9 ... His exaltation predicted ... Acts 1 :11 ;Eph. 1 :20
Psa. 100:5 ... His character-Goodness ... Mt. 19:16, 17
Psa. 102:1–11 ... The Suffering and Reproach of Calvary ... Jn. 21:16-30
Psa. 102:25–27 ... Messiah is the Preexistent Son ... Heb. 1 :10–12
Psa. 109:25 ... Ridiculed ... Mt. 27: 39
Psa. 110:1 ... Son of David ... Mt. 22:43
Psa. 110:1 ... To ascend to the right-hand of the Father. .. Mk.16:19
Psa. 110:1 ... David's son called Lord ... Mt. 22:44,45
Psa. 110:4 ... A priest after Melchizedek's order ... Heb. 6:20
Psa. 112:4 ... His character-Compassionate, Gracious, et al. .. Mt. 9;36
Psa. 118:17, 18 ... Messiah's Resurrection assured ... Lu. 24:5-7;1 Cor. 15:20
Psa. 118:22, 23 ... The rejected stone is Head of the corner ... Mt. 21:42,43
Psa. 118:26a ... The Blessed One presented to Israel. .. Mt. 21:9
Psa. 118:26b ... To come while Temple standing ... Mt. 21;12–15
Psa. 132: 11 ... The Seed of David (the fruit of His Body) ... Lu. 1:32
Psa. 138:1–6 ... The supremacy of David's Seed amazes kings ... Mt. 2:2-6
Psa. 147:3, 6 ... The earthly ministry of Christ described ... Lu. 4:18
Psa. 1:23 ... He will send the Spirit of God ... Jn. 16;7
Song. 5:16 ... The altogether lovely One ... Jn. 1:17
Isa. 6:1 ... When Isaiah saw His glory ... Jn. 12:40–41
Isa. 6:9–10 ... Parables fall on deaf ears ... Mt. 13:13–15
Isa. 6:9–12 ... Blinded to Christ and deaf to His words ... Acts. 28:23–29
Isa. 7:14 ... To be born of a virgin ... Lu. 1:35
Isa. 7:14 ... To be Emmanuel—God with us ... Mt. 1:18-23
Isa. 8:8 ... Called Emmanuel. .. Mt. 28:20
Isa. 8:14 ... A stone of stumbling, a Rock of offense ... 1 Pet. 2:8
Isa. 9:1, 2 ... His ministry to begin in Galilee ... Mt. 4:12–17
Isa. 9:6 ... A child born—Humanity ... Lu. 1:31
Isa. 9:6 ... A Son given—Deity ... Lu. 1:32; Jn. 1;14; 1 Tim. 3:16
Isa. 9:6 ... Declared to be the Son of God with power ... Rom. 1 :3,4
Isa. 9:6 ... The Wonderful One, Peleh ... Lu. 4:22
Isa. 9:6 ... The Counsellor, Yaatz ... Mt. 13:54
Isa. 9:6 ... The Mighty God, El Gibor ... Mt. 11:20

Isa. 9:6 ... The Everlasting Father, Avi Adth ... Jn. 8:58
Isa. 9:6 ... The Prince of Peace, Sar Shalom ... Jn . 16:33
Isa. 9:7 ... To establish an everlasting kingdom ... Lu. 1:32-33
Isa. 9:7 ... His Character—Just ... Jn. 5:30
Isa. 9:7 ... No end to his Government, Throne, and Peace ... Lu. 1:32–33
Isa. 11:1 ... Called a Nazarene—the Branch, Natzar ... Mt. 2:23
Isa. 11:1 ... A rod out of Jesse—Son of Jesse ... Lu. 3:23,32
Isa. 11:2 ... The anointed One by the Spirit ... Mt. 3;16,17
Isa. 11:2 ... His Character—Wisdom, Understanding, et al. ... Jn. 4:4–26
Isa. 11:4 ... His Character—Truth ... Jn. 14:6
Isa. 11:10 ... The Gentiles seek Him ... Jn. 12:18–21
Isa. 12:2 ... Called Jesus—Yeshua ... Mt. 1:21
Isa. 25:8 ... The Resurrection predicted ... 1 Cor. 15:54
Isa. 26:19 ... His power of Resurrection predicted ... Jn. 11 :43, 44
Isa. 28:16 ... The Messiah is the precious corner stone ... Acts 4:11, 12
Isa. 29:13 ... He indicated hypocritical obedience to His Word ... Mt. 15:7–9
Isa. 29:14 ... The wise are confounded by the Word ... I Cor. 1: 18–31
Isa. 32:2 ... A Refuge—A man shall be a hiding place ... Mt. 23:37
Isa. 35:4 ... He will come and save you ... Mt. 1:21
Isa. 35:5 ... To have a ministry of miracles ... Mt. 11:4–6
Isa. 40:3, 4 ... Preceded by forerunner ... Jn. 1:23
Isa. 40:9 ... "Behold your God." ... Jn. 1:36; 19:14
Isa. 40:11 ... A shepherd—compassionatelife-giver ... Jn. 10:10–18
Isa. 42:1–4 ... The Servant—as a faithful, patient redeemer ... Mt.12:18–21
Isa. 42:2 ... Meek and lowly ... Mt. 11 :28–30
Isa. 42:3 ... He brings hope for the hopeless ... Jn. 4
Isa. 42:4 ... The nations shall wait on His teachings ... Jn. 12:20–26
Isa. 42:6 ... The Light (salvation) of the Gentiles ... Lu. 2:32
Isa. 42:1,6 ... His is a Worldwide compassion ... Mt. 28: 19,20
Isa. 42:7 ... Blind eyes opened ... Jn. 9:25–38
Isa. 43:11 ... He is the only Saviour ... Acts. 4:12
Isa. 44:3 ... He will send the Spirit of God ... Jn. 16:7, 13
Isa. 45:23 ... He will be the Judge ... Jn. 5:22;Rom. 14:11
Isa. 48:12 ... The First and the Last ... Jn. 1:30;Rev. 1:8, 17
Isa. 48:17 ... He came as a Teacher ... Jn. 3:2
Isa. 49:1 ... Called from the womb-His humanity ... Mt. 1 :18
Isa. 49:5 ... A Servant from the womb ... Lu. 1:31; Phil. 2:7
Isa. 49:6 ... He is Salvation for Israel. ... Lu. 2:29–32
Isa. 49:6 ... He is the Light of the Gentiles ... Acts 13:47

Isa. 49:6 ... He is Salvation unto the ends of the earth ... Acts 15:7–18
Isa. 49:7 ... He is despised of the Nation ... Jn. 8:48–49
Isa. 50:3 ... Heaven is clothed in black at His humiliation ... Lu. 23:44, 45
Isa. 50:4 ... He is a learned counsellor for the weary ... Mt. 11 :28, 29
Isa. 50:5 ... The Servant bound willingly to obedience ... Mt. 26:39
Isa. 50:6a ... "I gave my back to the smiters." ... Mt. 27:26
Isa. 50:6b ... He was smitten on the cheeks ... Mt. 26:67
Isa. 50:6c ... He was spat upon ... Mt. 27:30
Isa. 52:7 ... To publish good tidings of peace ... Lu. 4:14, 15
Isa. 52:13 ... The Servant exalted ... Acts 1:8-11; Eph. 1:19–22
Isa. 52:13 ... Behold, My Servant. .. Mt. 17:5; Phil. 2:5–8
Isa. 52:14 ... The Servant shockingly abused ... Lu. 18:31–34; Mt. 26:67, 68
Isa. 52:15 ... Nations startled by message of the Servant ... Rom. 15: 18–21
Isa. 52:15 ... His blood shed to make atonement for all. .. Rev. 1: 5
Isa. 53:1 ... His people would not believe Him ... Jn. 12:37–38
Isa. 53:2a ... He would grow up in a poor family .... Lu. 2:7
Isa. 53:2b ... Appearance of an ordinary man ... Phil. 2:7-8
Isa. 53:3a ... Despised .... Lu. 4:28–29
Isa. 53:3b ... Rejected ... Mt. 27:21–23
Isa. 53:3c ... Great sorrow and grief ... Lu. 19:41–42
Isa. 53:3d ... Men hide from being associated with Him ... Mk. 14:50–52
Isa. 53:4a ... He would have a healing ministry ... Lu. 6:17–19
Isa. 53:4b ... He would bear the sins of the world ... 1 Pet. 2:24
Isa. 53:4c. .. Thought to be cursed by God ... Mt. 27:41–43
Isa. 53:5a ... Bears penalty for mankind's transgressions ... Lu. 23:33
Isa. 53:5b ... His sacrifice would provide peace between man and God ... Col. 1:20
Isa. 53:5c ... His back would be whipped ... Mt. 27:26
Isa. 53:6a ... He would be the sin-bearer for all mankind ... Gal. 1 :4
Isa. 53:6b ... God's will that He bear sin for all mankind ... 1 Jn. 4:10
Isa. 53:7a ... Oppressed and afflicted ... Mt. 27:27–31
Isa. 53:7b ... Silent before his accusers ... Mt. 27:12–14
Isa. 53:7c ... Sacrificial lamb ... Jn. 1 :29
Isa. 53:8a ... Confined and persecuted ... Mt. 26:47–27:31
Isa. 53:8b ... He would be judged ... Jn. 18: 13–22
Isa. 53:8c ... Killed .... Mt. 27:35
Isa. 53:8d ... Dies for the sins of the world ... 1 Jn. 2:2
Isa. 53:9a ... Buried in a rich man's grave ... Mt. 27:57
Isa. 53:9b ... Innocent and had done no violence ... Mk. 15:3
Isa. 53:9c ... No deceit in his mouth ... Jn. 18:38

Isa. 53:10a ... God's will that He die for mankind ... Jn. 18:11
Isa. 53:10b ... An offering for sin ... Mt. 20:28
Isa. 53:10c ... Resurrected and live forever .... Mk. 16:16
Isa. 53:10d ... He would prosper ... Jn. 17:1–5
Isa. 53:11 a ... God fully satisfied with His suffering ... Jn. 12:27
Isa. 53:11b ... God's servant ... Rom. 5:18–19
Isa. 53:11c ... He would justify man before God ... Rom. 5:8–9
Isa. 53:11d ... The sin-bearer for all mankind ... Heb. 9:28
Isa. 53:12a ... Exalted by God because of his sacrifice ... Mt. 28:18
Isa. 53:12b ... He would give up his life to save mankind ... Lu. 23:46
Isa. 53:12c ... Grouped with criminals ... Lu. 23:32
Isa. 53:12d ... Sin-bearer for all mankind ... 2 Cor. 5:21
Isa. 53:12e ... Intercede to God in behalf of mankind ... Lu. 23:34
Isa. 55:3 ... Resurrected by God ... Acts 13:34
Isa. 55:4 ... A witness ... Jn. 18:37
Isa. 59:15–16a ... He would come to provide salvation ... Jn. 6:40
Isa. 59:15–16b ... Intercessor between man and God ... Mt. 10:32
Isa. 59:20 ... He would come to Zion as their Redeemer ... Lu. 2:38
Isa. 61:1–2a ... The Spirit of God upon him ... Mt. 3:16–17
Isa. 61:1–2b ... The Messiah would preach the good news ... Lu. 4: 17–21
Isa. 61:1–2c ... Provide freedom from the bondage of sin and death ... Jn. 8:31–32
Isa. 61:1–2 ... Proclaim a period of grace ... Jn. 5:24
Jer.23:5–6a ... Descendant of David ... Lu. 3:23–31
Jer. 23:5–6b ... The Messiah would be God ... Jn. 13:13
Jer. 23:5–6c ... The Messiah would be both God and Man ... 1 Tim. 3:16
Jer. 31:22 ... Born of a virgin ... Mt. 1:18–20
Jer. 31:31 ... The Messiah would be the new covenant ... Mt. 26:28
Jer. 33:14–15 ... Descendant of David ... Lu. 3:23–31
Eze. 17:22–24 ... Descendant of David ... Lk. 3:23–31
Eze. 34:23–24 ... Descendant of David ... Mt. 1:1
Dan. 7:13–14a ... He would ascend into heaven ... Acts 1 :9–11
Dan. 7: 13–14b ... Highly exalted ... Eph. 1:20–22
Dan. 7:13–14c ... His dominion would be everlasting ... Lu. 1:31–33
Dan. 9:24a ... To make an end to sins ... Gal. 1 :3–5
Dan. 9:24b ... He would be holy ... Lu. 1:35
Dan. 9:25 ... Announced to his people 483 years, to the exact day, after the decree to rebuild the city of Jerusalem ... Jn. 12:12–13
Dan. 9:26a ... Killed ... Mt. 27:35
Dan. 9:26b ... Die for the sins of the world ... Heb. 2:9

Dan. 9:26c ... Killed before the destruction of the temple ... Mt. 27:50-51
Dan. 10:5-6 ... Messiah in a glorified state ... Rev. 1:13-16
Hos. 13:14 ... He would defeat death ... 1 Cor. 15:55-57
Joel 2:32 ... Offer salvation to all mankind ... Rom. 10:12-13
Mic. 5:2a ... Born in Bethlehem ... Mt. 2:1-2
Mic. 5:2b ... God's servant ... Jn. 15:10
Mic. 5:2c ... From everlasting ... Jn. 8:58
Hag. 2:6-9 ... He would visit the second Temple ... Lu. 2:27-32
Hag. 2:23 ... Descendant of Zerubbabel. .. Lu. 3:23-27
Zech. 3:8 ... God's servant ... Jn. 17:4
Zech. 6:12-13 ... Priest and King ... Heb. 8:1
Zech. 9:9a ... Greeted with rejoicing in Jerusalem ... Mt. 21 :8-10
Zech. 9:9b ... Beheld as King ... Jn. 12:12-13
Zech. 9:9c ... The Messiah would be just ... Jn. 5:30
Zech. 9:9d ... The Messiah would bring salvation ... Luke 19:10
Zech. 9:9e ... The Messiah would be humble ... Mt. 11:29
Zech. 9:9f ... Presented to Jerusalem riding on a donkey ... Mt. 21:6-9
Zech. 10:4 ... The cornerstone ... Eph. 2:20
Zech. 11:4-6a ... At His coming, Israel to have unfit leaders ... Mt. 23:1-4
Zech. 11:4-6b ... Rejection causes God to remove His protection .. Lu. 19:41-44
Zech. 11:4-6c ... Rejected in favor of another king ... Jn. 19:13-15
Zech. 11:7 ... Ministry to "poor," the believing remnant ... Mt. 9:35-36
Zech. 11:8a ... Unbelief forces Messiah to reject them ... Mt. 23:33
Zech. 11:8b ... Despised ... Mt. 27:20
Zech. 11:9 ... Stops ministering to the those who rejected Him ... Mt. 13:10-11
Zech. 11:10-11 a ... Rejection causes God to remove protection ... Lu. 19:41-44
Zech. 11:10-11 b ... The Messiah would be God ... Jn. 14:7
Zech. 11:12-13a ... Betrayed for thirty pieces of silver ... Mt. 26:14-15
Zech. 11:12-13b ... Rejected ... Mt. 26:14-15
Zech. 11:12-13c ... Thirty pieces of silver thrown into the house of the Lord ... Mt. 27:3-5
Zech. 11:12-13d ... The Messiah would be God ... Jn. 12:45
Zech. 12:10a ... The Messiah's body would be pierced ... Jn. 19:34-37
Zech. 12:10b .. The Messiah would be both God and man ... Jn. 10:30
Zech. 12:10c ... The Messiah would be rejected ... Jn. 1:11
Zech. 13:7a ... God's will He die for mankind ... Jn. 18:11
Zech. 13:7b ... A violent death ... Mt. 27:35
Zech. 13:7c ... Both God and man .. Jn. 14:9
Zech. 13:7d ... Israel scattered as a result of rejecting Him ... Mt. 26:31-56

Mal. 3:1a ... Messenger to prepare the way for Messiah ... Mt. 11:10
Mal. 3:1b ... Sudden appearance at the temple ... Mk. 11: 15-16
Mal. 3:1c ... Messenger of the new covenant ... Lu. 4:43
Mal. 4:5 ... Forerunner in the spirit of Elijah ... Mt. 3:1-2
Mal. 4:6 ... Forerunner would turn many to righteousness ... Lu. 1 :16-17

Bible Prophecy
Christ in the Old Testament

NEW TESTAMANT—LUKE

Matt. 27:35; Luke 24:39–40 Luke 3:36	Gen. 3:15
Luke 3:34	Gen. 9:26–27
Luke 2:1–7; Gal. 4:4	Gen. 28:14
Luke 3:33	Gen. 49:10
Luke 1:35; Acts 4:27	Ex. 15:11
Luke 1:72	Ex. 33:19
Luke 5:12–14; Acts 6:7	Lev. 14:11
Luke 1:32; Romans 1:3–4	1 Sam. 7:14a
Luke 3:31; Rev. 22:16	1 Sam. 7:16
Luke 24:51	2 Kings 2:11
Luke 1:32–33	1 Chr. 17:12–13
Luke 24:6	Psa. 17:15
Luke 1:69–71	Psa. 18:2–3
Luke 2:7	Psa. 22:9–10
Luke 23:34–35	Psa. 22:17–18
Luke 19:23–24	Psa. 22:18
Luke 23:46	Psa. 22:20–21
Luke 23:46	Psa. 22:31:5
Luke 23:49	Psa. 38:11
John 1:17; Luke 4:22	Psa. 45:2
Luke 2:11	Psa. 45:7–8
Luke 24:51	Psa. 68:18
Luke 23:49	Psa. 88:8
Luke 1:32–33	Psa. 89:27
Luke 1:32–33	Psa. 89:35–37
Luke 4:10–11	Psa. 91:11–12
Luke 24:5–7; 1 Cor. 15:20	Psa. 118:17–18
Luke 1:32; Acts 2:30	Psa. 132:11
Luke 4:18	Psa. 147:3, 6
Luke 1:35	Isa. 7:14
Luke 1:31	Isa 9:6
Luke 1:32; John 1:14; 1 Tim 3:16	Isa. 9:6
Luke 4:22	Isa. 9:6
Luke 1:32–33	Isa. 9:7
Luke 1:32–33	Isa. 9:7

Luke 3:23,32	Isa. 11:1
Luke 6:8; John 2:25	Isa. 11:3
Luke 2:32	Isa. 42:6
Luke 1:31; Phil. 2:7	Isa. 49:5
Luke 2:29–32	Isa. 49:6
Luke 23:44–45	Isa. 50:3
Luke 18:31–34; Mt. 26:67–68	Isa. 52:14
Luke 18:31–34; Mt. 26:67–68	Isa. 52:15
Luke 4:28–29	Isa. 53:3a
Matt. 26:37–38; Luke 19:41; Hebrews 4:15	Isa. 53:3c
Luke 23:41; John 18:38	Isa. 53:9b
Luke 23:46	Isa. 53:12b
Luke 23:34; Romans 8:34	Isa. 53:12e
Luke 2:38	Isa. 59:20
Luke 4:16–21	Isa. 61:1b
Luke 3:23–31	Jer. 23:5–6
Luke 3:23–31	Jer. 33:14–15
Luke 1:31–33	Eze. 37:24–25
Luke 1:31–33	Dan. 7:13–14c
Luke 1:35	Dan. 9:24c
Luke 1:33	Mic. 5:2b
Luke 2:27–32	Hag. 2:6–9
Luke 2:27–32	Hag. 2:23
Luke 19:10	Zech. 9:9d
Luke 19:41–44	Zech. 11:4–6b
Luke 19:41–44	Zech. 11:10–11a
Luke 4:43	Mal. 3:1c
Luke 1:16–17	Mal. 4:6

NEW TESTAMANT—JOHN

Hebrews 2:14; 1 John 3:8	Gen. 3:15
John 1:29	Gen. 22:8
John 1:51	Gen. 28:12
John 17:3	Gen. 49:10
John 11:47–52	Gen. 49:10
John 10:16	Gen. 49:10
John 4:26, 8:58	Ex. 3:13–15
John 19:31–36	Ex. 12:46
John 7:37	Lev. 23:36–37
John 19:31–36	Num. 9:12

John 3:14–18, 12:32	Num. 21:9
John 1:14; Galatians 4:4	Num. 24:17
John 6:14	Deut. 18:15
John 5:45–47	Deut. 18:15
John 8:28–29	Deut. 18:18
Mt. 28:18; John 12:15	1 Sam. 2:10
John 5:24–29	Job 19:23–37
John 1:41; Acts 2:36	Psa. 2:2
John 8:46; Revelation 3:7	Psa. 2:6
John 20:31	Psa. 2:12
John 20:9	Psa. 16:9–11
John 19:6	Psa. 22:12–13
John 19:34	Psa. 22:14
John 19:28	Psa. 22:15
John 19:34, 37, 20:27	Psa. 22:16
John 20:17	Psa. 22:22
John 19:30; Heb. 10:10, 12, 14, 18	Psa. 22:31
John 10:11; 1 Peter 2:25	Psa. 23:1
Mt. 27:1; John 11:53	Psa. 31:13
John 19:31–36	Psa. 31:13
John 15:25	Psa. 35:19
John 20:20	Psa. 40:2–5
John 4:34; Heb. 10:5–10	Psa. 40:6–8
John 18:4–6	Psa. 40:14
John 13:18	Psa. 41:9
John 1:17; Luke 4:22	Psa. 45:2
John 13:18	Psa. 41:9
John 15:25	Psa. 45:2
John 1:11, 7:5	Psa. 55:12–14
John 2:17	Psa. 69:9
John 17:4, 18–11	Psa. 69:26
John 12:24–25	Psa. 72:16
John 1:12–13	Psa. 72:17
John 12:13; Rev. 5:8–12	Psa. 72:17
John 1:1	Psa. 90:2
John 19:16–17	Psa. 102:1–11
John 16:7	Prov. 1:23
John 1:17	Song. 5:16
John 4:25	Isa. 2:3
John 5:25	Isa. 2:4

John 12:40–41	Isa. 6:1
John 12:38–45	Isa. 6:8
Luke 1:32; John 1:14; 1 Tim 3:16	Isa. 9:6
John 8:58, 10:30	Isa. 9:6
John 16:33	Isa. 9:6
John 5:30	Isa. 9:7
Luke 6:8; John 2:25	Isa. 11:13
John 12:18–21	Isa. 11:10
John 1:23	Isa. 40:3–4
John 1:36, 19:14	Isa. 40:9
John 10:10–18	Isa. 40:11
John 4:1–26	Isa 42:3
John 12:20–26	Isa. 42:4
John 9:25–38	Isa. 42:7
John 16:7, 13	Isa. 44:3
John 5:22; Romans 14:11	Isa. 45:23
John 13:19	Isa. 46:9–10
John 1:30; Rev. 1:8, 17	Isa. 48:12
John 3:2	Isa. 48:16
John 8:12; Acts 13:47	Isa. 49:6
John 1:11, 8:48–49, 19:14–15	Isa. 49:7
John 12:37–38	Isa. 53:1
John 1:29; 1 Peter 1:18–19	Isa. 53:7c
John 18:13–22	Isa. 53:8b
Luke 23:41; John 18:38	Isa. 53:9b
John 18:11	Isa. 53:10a
John 17:1–5	Isa. 53:10d
John 12:27	Isa. 53:11a
John 18:37	Isa. 55:4a
John 6:40	Isa. 59:16b
John 8:31–36	Isa. 61:1c
John 13:13; 1 Titus 3:16	Jer. 23:5–6
John 12:12–13	Dan. 9:25
John 8:58, 10:30	Mic. 5:2c
John 17:4, 18–11	Zech. 3:8
John 12:12–13	Zech. 9:9b
John 5:30	Zech. 9:9c
John 19:13–15	Zech. 99:4–6c
John 14:7	Zech. 11:10–11b

John 12:45	Zech. 11:12–13d
John 19:34–37	Zech. 12:10a
John 10:30	Zech. 12:10b
John 1:11	Zech. 12:10c
John 18:11	Zech. 13:7a
John 14:9	Zech. 13:7c

NEW TESTAMENT—ACTS

Gal. 3:8; Acts 3:25–26	Gen. 12:3
Acts 7:55–56	Ex. 15:2–15
Luke 1:35; Acts 4:27	Ex. 15:11
Luke 5:12–14; Acts 6:7	Lev. 14:11
Acts 3:22–23	Deut. 18:19
Acts 4:25–28	Psa. 2:1–3
John 1:41; Acts 2:36	Psa. 2:2
Acts 13:29–33	Psa. 2:7–8
Acts 17:31	Psa. 9:7–10
Acts 2:31, 13:35	Psa. 16:10
Acts 1:11; Philippians 2:9	Psa. 24:3
Acts 2:32	Psa. 30:3
Acts 10:38	Psa. 38:20
Matt. 27:3–5; Acts 1:16–19	Psa. 55:15
Acts 1:11; Ephesians 1:20	Psa. 97:9
Luke 1:32; Acts 2:30	Psa. 132:11
Acts 28:23–29	Isa. 6:9–12
Matt. 3:16–17; Acts 10:38	Isa. 11:2
Acts 17:31	Isa. 11:4
Acts 4:11–12	Isa. 28:16
Acts 4:12	Isa. 43:11
Acts 3:19–21, 15:16–17	Isa. 49:6
John 8:12; Acts 13:47	Isa. 49:6
Acts 15:7–18	Isa. 49:6
Acts 1:8–11; Eph. 1:19–22; Phil. 2:5–9	Isa. 52:13
Acts 13:34	Isa. 55:3
Acts 3:13	Isa. 55:5
Acts 26:23	Isa. 60:1–3
Acts 1:9–11	Dan. 7:13–14a
Acts 1:11–12	Zech. 14:4

NEW TESTAMENT—ROMANS

Romans 9:7	Gen. 17:29
Romans 5:8	Ex. 12:13
Romans 3:23–24; 1 John 1:7	Lev. 17:11
Luke 1:32; Romans 1:3–4	1 Sam. 7:14a
Matt. 3:17; Romans 1:4	Psa. 2:7
Romans 1:3–4	Isa. 9:6
John 5:22; Romans 14:11	Isa. 45:23
Romans 6:9	Isa. 53:10c
Romans 5:8–9, 18–19	Isa. 53:11b
Luke 23:34; Romans 8:34	Isa. 53:12e
Rom. 5:10; 2 Cor. 5:18–21	Dan. 9:24b
Romans 10:9–13	Joel 2:32

NEW TESTAMENT—1 CORINTHIANS

1 Corinthians 10:4	Ex. 12:21–27
1 Corinthians 10:4	Ex. 17:6
Luke 24:5–7; 1 Cor. 15:20	Psa. 118:17–18
1 Cor. 1:24; Titus 2:3	Isa. 9:6
1 Corinthians 15:54	Isa. 25:8
1 Cor. 3:11; Mt 16:18	Isa. 28:16
1 Corinthians 1:18–31	Isa. 29:14
1 Corinthians 15:15–57	Hos. 13:14

NEW TESTAMENT—2 CORINTHIANS

2 Corinthians 5:21	Psa. 22:1
2 Cor. 5:21; Heb 2:9	Isa. 53:5a
Rom. 5:10; 2 Cor. 5:18–21	Dan. 9:24b

www.ingramcontent.com/pod-product-compliance
Lightning Source LLC
LaVergne TN
LVHW020058090426
835510LV00040B/2446